The Art and Science of Security Risk Assessment

IRA S. SOMERSON, CPP

ASIS
INTERNATIONAL
Advancing Security Worldwide®

Dedicated to the warm and
wonderful world of my wife, Beverly

The Art and Science of Risk Assessment

Acknowledgments

- In appreciation and memory of **William J. Stevenson,** my commanding officer, first employer in private security, and professional mentor.

- **Robert M. Figlio, Ph.D.** (CAP Index, Inc., Exton, PA) for his assistance with preparing Chapter 7, Demographic Analysis in Risk Assessment. Dr. Figlio passed away in April, 2008. He will always be remembered for his significant intellectual and academic support to the Security Management Industry.

- **Brian McIlravey, CPP,** (PPM 2000, Inc., Edmonton, Alberta Canada) for his assistance with preparing Chapter 6, Incident Reporting and Incident Data Management.

- **Rick Shaw,** (Awareity, Inc., Washington, DC), for his assistance with preparing Chapter 8, Internal and Human Factor Controls.

- **David L. Johnston, CPP,** for his support and vigorous review and insight with the development of this text.

- **James M. Dallas, CPP,** for his support and vigorous review and insight with the development of this text.

- **ASIS International** staff and educational programming. The cumulative knowledge imparted over my 45 years of membership were invaluable to the context of my project.

- **International Association of Professional Security Consultants (IAPSC),** for the peer review and support with this project.

Contents

Chapter Two: The Nature of Risk

Chapter Three: Convergence as It Applies to Risk Assessment

Chapter Four: Security Surveys - A Strategic Function of Risk Assessment

Chapter Five: Risk Assessment by Focus Group

Chapter Six: Incident Reporting and Incident Data Management

Chapter Seven: Demographic Analysis in Risk Assessment

Chapter Eight: Internal and Human Factor Controls

Preface

When I first went to work in the private security industry in 1959, I had just been discharged from the U.S. Navy. I was invited to join a regional security service company owned and operated by my former commanding officer who served with the Office of Naval Intelligence. His security service agency was providing security officer services and business investigations. These services were entirely different from today's generation as they fulfilled the security needs of a very different clientele. Security services in the 1950s primarily focused on industries doing business with the U.S. Government, a vestige of World War II and its economy. Security officers were assigned to manufacturing facilities (primarily aerospace), military bases, and other ancillary government agency buildings to provide access control. Other services included fire prevention and perimeter patrol, bur rarely were these services performed as a response to the assessment of the overall risks to the organization. The closest to this would have been a response to a specific threat occasioned by an incident. The most significant percentage of investigative services involved preemployment screening as a precursor to candidates for employment requiring government secret clearance.

Policy and procedures for security strategies were essentially guided by the Industrial Security Defense Manual (ISDM). The enormous industrial growth spawned by World War II created new business opportunities and the beginning of America's consumerism. In the late 1950s new competitive industries were born. Security began to support an entirely new management paradigm. Retired federal agents and military intelligence officers filled key security positions concerned with managing and protecting information for companies having classified contracts with the United States Government. Corporate business management was still evolving as America's industries changed from war effort industrialization to sating the needs of consumerism in an entirely new competitive marketplace. Security practitioners were primarily known to have come from military intelligence agencies, federal, state or local law enforcement agencies. It was a small, but tight discipline. It was in this time period that these practitioners formed the American Society for Industrial Security (1955).

The 1960s brought a different experience to the traditional law enforcement stereotype. It was a time of social dissent. The civil rights and anti-war movements were two of many challenges facing law enforcement and security practitioners. Liberalism and political activism challenged the very core of conventional law enforcement agenda. Business, and in particular, the American college campus began to feel the brunt of this change. It challenged old values and raised serious concerns about how assets could be protected while social change took its course. Business, government, and institutions now sought to maintain law and order in their respective environments. Law enforcement was recruited by business to protect their investment and it was not until the 1970s and the end of the Vietnam conflict that this role began to change again.

The beginning of the 1970s saw the start of a new national priority, law, and order. The Law Enforcement Assistance Administration (LEAA) was created and large grants were provided for funding research that studied the problems of the criminal justice system and educating America's law enforcement community. The Rand Report and LEAA's Study titled *"Private Security"* were landmark studies which, to a large extent, criticized the security industry. The *Hallcrest Report* spelled out the failings of the law enforcement community and corporate/private security to work together in achieving the objectives of crime prevention. It was during this decade that many law enforcement practitioners got their college education and a chance to change and improve their careers. College educated law enforcement supervisors retired from federal, state, and local assignments and entered the business world in varying security management assignments. The business community perceived that these men and women were the ones qualified to manage their security risks. Business, for the most part, considered that these professionals understood what risks needed to be managed. As long as things remained under control and they were not required to make undue investments in security, the status-quo existed. Business still felt that the investigative and protection skills of law enforcement officers were what was needed to fulfill their agenda. Some industries did begin to recognize the importance of adding security management to their strategic planning, but they were the exception rather than the rule. Retailing, pharmaceuticals, utilities and banking were some of the industries that began to recognize the importance of developing pro-active security management programs and integrating it with the balance of management.

The growth of the security industry during the 1970s, both proprietary and contract services, was enormous. It was during this period that major capital investments in technology occurred and extraordinary improvements in security hardware evolved. Miniaturization, computerization, and the start of the "Information Age" were now part of the business lexicon. It was also a time when national security officer services went national. Later in the 1970s we began to see the start of specialization in the security industry. The complexities of each industry and/or the multitude of varying defensive strategies made it necessary for security practitioners to confine themselves to the special security applications of their respective expertise. Professional and trade associations, within each security discipline, met to share information and network. Security managers in groups such as banking, retailing, and pharmaceutical industries met to discuss problems that concerned their particular vulnerabilities. The same was true of vendors who provided services.

The survivors of the 1970s are those security managers who recognized the need to become professional business managers. They sought parity from management by earning the same degrees, learning to communicate as business persons, and earned the respect and acceptance of senior management. Unfortunately, this did not constitute a major movement.

Intelligence investigations, for many years, involved the manual analysis of data. Analysts would work to identify relational significance in small rooms surrounded by black boards filled with copious notes and cork boards pinned with an array of 3" x 5" cards. Today's investigator enters unrelated intelligence into their computer database which then conducts a global search of vast relational data from other databases to develop usable intelligence in seconds; once taking days or weeks. Just a few years ago, no one knew what "data mining" meant. Alarm systems, closed circuit television and access control are now managed by central processing units.

There was a time (and not too long ago) when business only had to cope with the competitive pressures of other domestic companies. In a few short years, the world shrunk and most industries now face a global marketplace. Businesses are not only concerned with the ethics and mores of a domestic environment, but must deal with the values of a dynamic world market. Vast new technologies in communications have placed enormous pressures on business to protect their data and the assets that pass through these technologies. The luxury of open academic environments for high-tech research must now cope with this same information being shared with tomorrow's potential foreign threat. Not only is this information exposed to foreign and terroristic threat, but by competitive intelligence gathering in the heated domestic and global market. Foreign travel by business executives places new threats upon the welfare of companies as their executives travel abroad to do business in countries embroiled in the terrorism and political extremism of third world countries.

As traditional threats of fraud and violations of corporate trust continued, new risks evolved from the dependency upon information technology. Many corporate resources became vulnerable in ways that typical law enforcement was not qualified to deal with. The 1980s saw assets disappear from companies' computer systems where no laws existed to protect those assets. With the passage of laws to protect these assets, business still waited for a new breed of law enforcement personnel to investigate these crimes and trained prosecutors willing to move this type of threat through the criminal justice system. The stage was set for skilled security practitioners who could pro-actively deal with these threats. But their efforts would achieve limited results unless they had the ability to encourage management to be part of the solution.

Until the 1990s American business had historically favored reactive security programs versus pro-active security management integrated with other operating units. This approach identified security risks by reacting to their occurrence rather than a careful analysis of their foreseeability and then planning for the management of same. Major business schools still energetically resisted including security management curricula that would heighten their students' awareness of crime's impact to profitability and viability. Risk Management curricula also did not include security risk assessment curricula. Matriculating students entered the business world never having any studied appreciation of the many facets of corporate criminality and exposure to intrinsic security threats. It is still left to the security practitioner within an organization to provide this important awareness, but because it wasn't presented in the business school they attended it lacks affirmation and credibility.

The typical reluctance of Americans to become involved in crime prevention doesn't change when they move to the corporate culture. Americans have long relied upon law enforcement to prevent crime in their communities and, unfortunately, most still think that law enforcement can manage security risk in their organizations. It is these same Americans in the business world who fail to recognize the intrinsic benefit and net present value of including a professionally managed security program.

Traditional security practitioners could not challenge this impasse. They came from a background where it was both patriotic and appropriate for leadership to define their role. They were imbued with the character of following orders. The 1990s saw a new type of security professional arrive on the scene. They were from business schools, law schools, and liberal arts programs. They have masters and doctoral degrees. Some are being recruited from within their company's business units. Many have never spent a day with a security responsibility and look to the line skills of their security organization for this technical support. They have been chosen as they are perceived as having the business and administration acumen to coordinate the security objective to the corporate strategic plan. They can identify and be accepted in this role where "the company cop" cannot achieve similar integration. Because they are not from a traditional security mold, they are more likely to challenge the status quo. Their stewardship of security management is considered a lateral or upward career move, not a fixed staff position. They will ensure that their agenda is shared with other management philosophy and mission so that they are not frozen out of the larger picture (the beginning of "convergence").

Where it was the Industrial Security Defense Manual that guided security strategies in the 1950s, it is now mandatory for security policy and procedures to identify and respond to foreseeable risks within an organization. Risks faced by business, such as 9/11, can no longer be ignored. The potential for failure, even fatality, is far too great. If *risk* has become the driver of security strategy, then the methodology for identifying and queuing these risks must also become a strategic business objective. Nevertheless, from 1959 to the present, many buyers of security services and products as well as those vendors providing technology and physical security services did so without making this critical analysis and paradigm shift. Current audits of business' security programs persistently find defensive strategies in place that bear no relationship to their foreseeable risks. The proximate cause of these failures are buyers of security services and products persistently using other criteria in making their buying decisions and vendors motivated by sales versus the intrinsic needs of their clients. These failures by business and vendors obfuscate the true objectives of security management and very often drive the costs for technology and other services to unnecessary levels. More importantly, they create a false sense of security and fail to establish a standard security practice (standard of care) that is responsive to intrinsic needs.

The Art and Science of Risk Assessment encourages the strategic necessity of prefacing security activity with risk assessment. This text is intended to assist in providing an effective guide to its implementation.

## CHAPTER ONE

Introduction

Depending upon many dynamics associated with your organization, failure to provide a *security risk assessment* prior to the development of a security program or upgrades to the existing program may constitute a violation of *standard security industry practices* (standard of care). An organization's understanding of this reality and developing the necessary strategies to conduct risk assessments will be a pivotal trend in the 21st century.

"Organizations exist in a constantly changing environment. Understanding the nature of change is important to understanding the changing environment as the source of risk to the organization"

"Strategic planning in organizations seems to go in and out of style, probably because the plans are drawn up in a vacuum without a good real-world understanding of the nature of change..."[1]

KEYWORDS

Risk, risk assessment, risk management, quantitative analysis, qualitative analysis, security management, vulnerability analysis, foreseeability, criticality (impact), queuing, standards, standard security practices (standard of care), net present value.

RATIONALE FOR RISK ASSESSMENT

The variety and causes of security risks are considerable. A security program's objectives are to deter, detect, delay, deny, respond to, and/or recover from reasonably foreseeable events. However, if a risk assessment lacks sufficient qualitative (unscientific) or quantitative (scientific) analysis, it probably will be considered below a standard security industry practice in an after-the-fact analysis.

---

1. *Business Risk Assessment,* Chapter 1, The Institute of Internal Auditors, David McNamee, CIA, CISA, SFE, CGFM, FIIA(M), 8/99.

"*Risk management* is a disciplined approach through which uncertain events can be identified, measured, and controlled to minimize loss and optimize the security returns on the investment dollar..."

"*Risk analysis remains the cornerstone of any security program, and it is the fastest way to gain a complete understanding of your organization's security profile—its strengths and weaknesses, its vulnerabilities and exposures.*" [2]

"Risk analysis includes risk assessment and risk management. These are different phases of making decisions based on risk. Risk assessment is a method of identifying and measuring risk. Risk management is taking action to minimize risk (including installing internal controls). **Risk Assessment** is the quantitative and qualitative evaluation of exposure arising from some activity. **Risk Management** is the process of determining whether or how much of the risk is acceptable and what action should be taken." [3]

STRATEGIC RISK

"Each work unit in the organization puts its assets to work through the management process and internal control systems. The work unit objectives are linked to the organization's over-all goals and objectives. Risk, in the form of uncertain changes in the environment, can affect the assets and/or the management process. The effects of risk depend also in part on the nature of the assets and the types of management processes and controls."[4]

Black's Law Dictionary defines **risk** as, "...the element of uncertainty in an undertaking; the possibility that actual future returns will deviate from expected returns. Risk may be moral, physical or economic."

Though seemingly grounded in the world of the actuarial sciences, *risk assessment* to a security professional has a different operational definition: *Risk Assessment* is the art and science of *identifying* security vulnerabilities; measuring the *likelihood* that each vulnerability will occur (foreseeability); *prioritizing* each identified vulnerability in comparison to all others identified (queuing); assessing the *opportunity* for a risk to occur; and measuring each vulnerability's *impact* upon the organization's assets (criticality). Senior management of many organizations assert that a security function

---

2. *Risk Analysis Without Pain,* Carol R. Hamilton, President, Expert Systems Software, ISPNews, January/February, 1992.
3. *Business Risk Assessment,* Chapter 2, p.1, The Institute of Internal Auditors, David McNamee, CIA, CISA, SFE, CGFM, FIIA(M), 8/99.
4. *Ibid.,* Chapter 2, p. 7.

is purely a cost center and does not produce any "net present value" (positive value of a strategy after the cost of defensive strategies have been implemented). Security departments and their operations are routinely downsized or eliminated exposing organizations to serious threats. Their objective is economy, but the very opposite will often occur.

"**Threat** is a combination of the risk, the consequence of that risk, and the likelihood that the negative event will take place. Threat is often used in analysis in place of the term "risk." The type of threat is actually an expression of the type of consequence: fire, flood, error, omission, delay, fraud, breakdown, obsolescence, and so forth. Threats come from the operation of risk in the environment, regardless of the controls or control environment." [5]

The responsibilities of security directors are evolving from "locks, bolts, and badges" (Felson, 1988) and perimeter protection to a more sophisticated involvement in organizational management. Confronted with novel, complex security exposures and attendant risks, traditional security functions are becoming only a part of the larger overall responsibilities of security directors. Given this evolution, the motivating problem of this paper is: What is the best approach to managing the growing complexity of corporate security threats so as to provide minimal security losses, for a particular level of investment in security? This paper argues that to provide an optimum level of security service to the organization not only must the security department be repositioned within the modern corporate but that its management requires the development of a new paradigm of organizing security functions. The approach taken here to developing such a paradigm focuses on demonstrating the weaknesses of a cost center management approach, which is considered representative of existing security management practices, and on advocating the strengths of moving toward a profit center management approach..."[6]

Why are organizations vulnerable to criticism of their security programs?

Organizations are reluctant to identify their risks and to document their failures. In conducting a risk assessment, efficient and economical software already exists to track and generate useful security incident data. The challenge is to create an organizational policy and procedure with senior management's strong support. This

---

5. *Ibid.,* Chapter 2, p. 8.
6. *A White Paper on a Value-Added Model for Security Management,* Stephen Gale, Keith Duncan, Rudolph Yaksick, John Tofflemire, Research Supported by the American Society for Industrial Security Foundation (ASIS), December, 1990.

ensures employees **will report** incidents the very first time they experience an incident or reasonable suspicion and analyze these data using a relational database.

Instead, senior management and counsel persistently avoid exposing their failures pointing to the concern of creating a self-incriminating record. In fact, failure to understand one's history and risks and promulgating same is the shortest route to culpability. If employees believe that their customers and their own best interests are served, they **will** support a well developed incident reporting and loss tracking program. Discovery and investigation will more often than not identify that organizations do **not** perform this vital risk assessment and are therefore doomed to persistent security incidents and possible liability.

Business managers are **not** taught security management (risk assessment) in business schools. They are exposed to "Risk Management." Most security problems are business and people problems, but still no serious undergraduate or graduate curriculum exist (within highly regarded **business** schools) to provide this important curricula to future business executives. As a result, an organization's strategic plan does **not include** and coordinate security oversight and program development. It is often left to others, not qualified to understand security risks, to assume this important stewardship. This could be an argument for hiring a security manager if an organization does have unique and developed security threats, but it also begs the issue of ensuring that other disciplines within an organization **integrate** analysis of security threats into their agenda (e.g. I.T., Risk Management, audit, safety/environmental, operations, human resources, legal, facilities, etc.) as they are routinely exposed to security issues.

WHY ORGANIZATIONS ARE VICTIMIZED

- Lack of strategic interest with security risk assessment and planning by senior executives
- Lack of adequate study of security risks
- Lack of commitment and investment in security strategies
- Deflecting the responsibility for security management to others (e.g. law enforcement or other corporate staff functions, etc.)
- Failing to understand the "net present value" of security management services

It is strategic that security program planners **know** the risks they are intending to mitigate or prevent and communicate these data to appropriate management. When your security program is responsive to intrinsic security risks, it has the potential for being perceived as an investment that produces a net present value.

DEFINITIONS FOR RISK

- **Legal:** The legal definition of Risk is the element of uncertainty in an undertaking.
- **Financial:** The Financial definition of Risk pertains to the ultimate cost to an organization for failing to identify vulnerabilities and develop deterrent/remedial programs.
- **Security:** "As used in the security profession: The possibility of loss resulting from a threat, security incident, or event." [7]

TYPES OF RISKS

- **Natural:** Natural Risks are those occasioned by everyday "acts of God" (e.g. floods, earthquakes, hurricanes, landslides, blizzards, etc.)
- **Man-made:** Man-made Risks are those occasioned through the purposeful or accidental acts of humans; they partially include:
  - **Commission:** Man-made acts that are committed purposely, such as sabotage, crime, etc.
  - **Acts of Omission:** The Man-made failure to do something that a person is required or expected to do.

There are five different types of risks with which organizations consistently must manage:

- **Dynamic risks**: Fluctuate under certain conditions such as weather or location.
- **Static risks:** These remain constant, without regard to other factors, such as regulations, laws, or standards.
- **Inherent risks:** These are sometimes unavoidable and are associated with a certain product, industry/business, location, or business operation.
- **Speculative risks:** Occur when an organization voluntarily subjects itself to a risky business operation.
- **Pure risks:** Natural disasters or criminal acts that do not fall into any of the above categories.

---

7. *General Security Risk Assessment Guideline,* p. 5, ASIS International 2003.

Inherent Risk

When you ask what is the primary risk in a convenience store operation, the usual answer is "robbery." Others may say shoplifting, but from the point of view of criticality and the potential for violence and/or loss of intrinsic assets, robbery would be the likely choice. Some will argue that not *all* convenience stores are vulnerable to robbery. This is true. But the fact remains that the basic operation of a convenience store (without adequate deterrents) makes it uniquely vulnerable to this particular crime. Although a bar and night club may also be vulnerable to a robbery, the response in this environment would probably be "aggravated or simple assault" (fighting). A department store? Shoplifting or fraud. A parking lot? Theft of/from auto. A high-rise residential building? Burglary and/or various assaults. Manufacturing? Process interruption, diversion, gray markets, product tampering, sabotage, etc. These examples are generalizations that require more study, but support why risk assessment and the identification of *inherent risks* is strategic in developing a security program. A security system should never be developed *solely* on the basis of anecdotal or experiential instincts. But studying potential inherent risks *should be* included in the risk assessment paradigm.

What are some of the resources we can use to identify *inherent risks*?

- **Research:** Most organizations are linked to a business, trade, or professional association. More often than not, these organizations have studied and/or published materials that identify unique risks in similar operations.
- **Legal Research:** Most industries and/or organizations have been the target of civil litigation or criminal prosecution. Database research with highly regarded search services can provide a wealth of data concerning an organization's vulnerabilities.
- **Underwriter Data:** Many organizations who have recognized their security risks have chosen to insure against its potential and purchased insurance rather than spread the risk or self-insure themselves. A risk management and/or underwriter's loss control department can be an excellent resource to identifying risk.

SOURCES OF RISK

- **Human factors:** probably the greatest single source of risk: human error/failure within an organization and threats from outside.
- **Mechanical factors:** are sources of risk resulting from reliance on some type of machinery, equipment, or technology.

- **Environmental factors:** include both design of the physical environment, weather, climate, social environment.
- **Procedural factors:** are those sources of risks caused by the use of certain procedures, routines, or operations.

SOURCES OF ASSET IDENTIFICATION

"Any individual within an organization can list assets, but such a list of the critical assets of the organization would probably fall considerably short of what is really critical. Individuals view assets based on their particular knowledge of the organization, their role or position in the organization, and what activities fall under their prescribed duties. Nevertheless, the asset owners are generally the most important source of information about the assets in need of protection." [8] Asset identification must always precede the risk assessment process.

RISK ASSESSMENT REQUIREMENTS

- A realization that there is a need for some type of assessment or evaluation to take place on a *scheduled* basis. This must be initiated and authorized at the senior management level.
- Adequate facilities, funds, equipment, personnel, and time for gathering necessary data and conducting analysis.
- A competent knowledge of the techniques for data collection that will be employed.
- A true desire on the part of management to see that the analysis/evaluation is done well.
- An agreed upon commitment to seeing that situations deserving change, brought to light by the analysis, are reasonably acted upon.

MEASUREMENTS

- **Validity:** Manner in which the analysis of determining risk is validated.
- **Reliability:** Reliability may be said to be the extent to which a measurement remains constant as it is repeated under conditions that are considered to be constant.

---

8. *Risk Management for Security Professionals,* Carl A. Roper, Butterworth-Heinemann, Chapter 4, pp. 34-35, 1999.

APPLICATIONS USED TO STUDY RISK

- **Qualitative (unscientific) Methodology.** These are strategies that attempt to identify the components of studies as opposed to the measurement of the components. "This approach employs two fundamental elements; the probability of an event occurring and the likely loss should it occur. Qualitative risk analysis makes use of a single figure produced from these elements. This is called the 'Annual Loss Expectancy (ALE)'. This is calculated for an event by simply multiplying the potential loss by the probability. It is thus theoretically possible to rank events in order of risk (ALE) and to make decisions based upon this. The problems with this type of risk analysis are usually associated with the unreliability and inaccuracy of the data. Probability can rarely be precise and can, in some cases, promote complacency. In addition, controls and countermeasures often tackle a number of potential events and the events themselves are frequently interrelated. Notwithstanding the drawbacks, a number of organizations have successfully adopted qualitative risk analysis." [9]

- **"Quantitative" (scientific) Methodology.** These are methodologies that attempt to measure the components of studies as opposed to the identity of the components. "This is by far the most widely used approach to risk analysis. Probability data is not required and only estimated potential loss is used. Most qualitative risk analysis methodologies make use of a number of interrelated elements." [10]

Examples of "Qualitative" Risk Assessment:

- Facility's perimeter and community surveys.
- Police Department and other community interviews.
- Employee and contractor interviews.
- Process and operational surveillance and studies.
- Analysis of existing physical and procedural security.

Examples of "Quantitative" Risk Assessment:

- Benchmarking all facilities operated by the organization to determine risk levels and a standard of care.

---

9. *Introduction to Risk Analysis, 2003, C & A Security Risk Analysis Group (www.security-risk-analysis. com/introduction.htm).*
10. *Ibid.*

- Benchmarking competitive or similar facilities to identify a standard of care.
- Analysis of public police (dispatch and/or incident data)
- Analysis of an organization's in-house incident data.
- Reference to and use of strategy (security practices) evolving from scientific research.
- Reference to and use of an existing body of knowledge.

What Should a Risk Assessment Consider?

- Perceptions of the facility and/or operation by the public.
- Perceptions of the facility and/or operation by its employees and contractors.
- Public statements and lifestyles of high-profile executives and employees.
- Demographics ("social disorder") of the community where the facility is located.
- Demographics of the facility's work force.
- Nature of neighboring properties.
- Access roads to the facility.
- Police and/or a facility's incident history.
- Facility management of its property and resources.
- Efficiency of a facility's existing security strategy.

RISK ASSESSMENT PROCESS

- **Survey:** A physical study, using formal instruments (e.g., survey form), to ascertain how that environment may be a contributor to the risk of assets.
- **Interviews:** Carefully constructed interviews with persons in the organization who, by experience or their knowledge of actual incidents of risk, can contribute to the risk assessment process.
- **Operational Reviews:** Using formal survey instruments, the study of an organization's *operation* (as a business or function) to determine how that operation may contribute to *inherent* or *foreseeable* risks to assets.
- **Ancillary Environments or Operations:** Using formal survey instruments, study the potential of what *other* business operations may contribute to the risk of assets.

- **Benchmark Study:** Using established benchmark methodology, assess the risks to assets attributable to other facilities in your organization and to *like, competitive, or other organizations in a geographically close proximity* to the target of your study.

Ingredients to a Risk Assessment Process

- Police criminal incident history (to include Uniform Crime Reporting Data).
- Intelligence from local, state, and federal agencies re threats.
- Organization's incident history to include complaints from third parties.
- Incident history of like, competitive, or, organizations having a close proximity to the studied location.
- Incident history from loss control inspections or loss prevention analysis by the organization's casualty underwriter.
- Prior litigation for inadequate security.
- Incident history of reports submitted to the organization's casualty underwriter.
- Incident history from other departmental record keeping involving risks to an organization's assets (e.g., Human Resources, Facilities, Legal, Finance; Safety, etc.).
- Use of Special Indexing and Research Reports: Certain risks are studied and measured as to their likelihood to occur when compared to all properties in a national, state, or county area.
- Focus Group Study: Facilitation of a cross-section of persons (focus group) in an organization to identify the likelihood, opportunity, and impact (criticality) of risks.

Prior Incident Data

Does a history of prior security incidents necessarily conclude that similar security incidents will occur again? What if the person(s) who committed the prior incidents were the only ones encouraged to do so? Other factors which encouraged the incidents did not exist and the perpetrators creating the prior incident history have now moved away from the area? Is it still foreseeable that the organization will have similar security incidents or will other organizations having predictive qualitative and quantitative factors be more likely? Clearly, prior incidents of security violations are corroborative of other factors, but prior incidents without looking at other factors may be misleading. Yet prior incident analysis has very often been used to identify foreseeability without evaluating other strategic factors.

ASSESSMENT MATRIX

"Matrix Approach: In Risk Assessment, an approach that matches system components with risks, threats or controls with the object of measuring and examining the combinations of the two axes." [11]

- **Probability:** In the Risk Assessment Matrix, probability is the *likelihood* of any particular undesirable event happening to an organization.

- **Opportunity:** What are the defensive strategies currently being used? Are these adequate or does their inadequacy add to the likelihood of a security risk occurring?

- **Criticality:** In the Risk Assessment Matrix, criticality is the *adversity or untoward effect (impact)* of any particular event happening to an organization.

ANALYTIC FRAMEWORK

The analytical framework of Risk Assessment may be viewed as several disparate questions. Thoughtful answers make up the parameters of proposed solutions or, perhaps, decisions to proceed with attempted solutions.

- **Cost-Benefit Analysis:** The evaluation of the cost of an occurrence measured against the cost of its prevention.

- **Ethical Analysis:** The evaluation of the ethical propriety of a particular deterrent program.

- **Institutional (Cultural) Analysis:** The evaluation of an organization's *cultural history* in order to ascertain if a deterrent program fits within its cultural boundaries and philosophy.

- **Legal Analysis:** An evaluation of a prospective deterrent program's legality from a civil/criminal law perspective.

- **Liability Analysis:** An evaluation of the prospective security program, in order to ascertain its likelihood to cause or attract liability litigation.

---

11. *Business Risk Assessment, Glossary,* p. 99, The Institute of Internal Auditors, David McNamee, CIA, CISA, SFE, CGFM, FIIA(M), 8/99.

Operational Impact

- **Direct Loss:** The impact caused by material "out-of-pocket" costs to an organization because of losses, damage, and/or replacement of physical item.

- **Asset Loss:** Cost accrued because of the loss of an asset.

- **Replacement Costs:** The costs to an organization resulting from the replacement of something.

- **People:** The costs to an organization resulting from the disruption or harm to people within the organizations or involved with the recovery of the loss.

- **Business Interruption:** The costs to an organization resulting from the disruption of normal business timing and operations.

- **Indirect Loss:** The very real, tangible damage suffered by a business organization's reputation in the marketplace, shareholder value, and/or the possibility of loss of market share or damaging civil litigation.

- **Reputation:** Events that have materially affected the business reputation of an organization (e.g. Exxon, Ford, Audi, etc.).

- **Market Share:** A companion to loss of reputation is loss of market share. However, loss of market is not always caused by loss of business reputation. Loss of market share can be caused by natural or man-made means that are quite beyond an organization's management to prevent.

- **Shareholder Value:** Loss of shareholder value can create serious financial loss to an organization's ability to raise capital or the value of its shareholder equity and net worth.

- **Liability:** Costly legal litigation can create an impact from several quarters.

- **Productivity:** Loss by employees having to defend a civil litigation. It can be very costly as well as detrimental to the business reputation of the organization.

RISK MANAGEMENT TECHNIQUES

- **Elimination***
  High Criticality
  High Probability

- **Reduction/Mitigation***
  High Probability
  Low to Moderate Criticality

*Historically, these are the areas under which security management (as well as risk management, life safety, etc.) would have stewardship, including, but not limited to:

Security/Safety Management Oversight
Crisis Management
Disaster Recovery, Planning & Training
Customer Protection
Personal Protection
Information Protection

- **Spreading Risk**
  High Criticality
  Low Probability
- **Risk Transfer** (Situational)
- **Insurance**
- **Assumption of Risk (Self Insurance/Acceptance)**
  Low Criticality
  Low Probability
- **Combination of Above Strategies**

Ongoing Program Assessment

- Purpose of Evaluation
- Efficiency/effectiveness of Risk Assessment
- Provide program feedback for validation
- Improve decision making
- Establish credibility

Evaluation Methods

- Process/program (result orientation)
- Outcome/measures (metrics)

STANDARD SECURITY PRACTICE

It is not enough for organizations to know how to respond to events and/or to expect that their presence alone will deter foreseeable acts. All physical and procedural security programs are *not* alike. They are different because their design should be responsive to deterring, detecting, delaying, denying, responding to, and/or recovering *from reasonably foreseeable events* in their environment. The fact that anomalous events do occur should not excuse or rationalize failing to perform adequate planning. It is inevitable that all risks will not be identified, but the very fact that a capable risk assessment was conduced puts an organization in a far more defensible posture. Colleagues may disagree as to the nature and degree of security strategies; this is why setting security "standards" is such a rocky road. *Conducting a risk assessment prior to implementing or upgrading a security program should be a standard security practice (standard of care) to which all security professionals should adhere.*

DOCUMENTATION

The deliverables from a security risk assessment are critical to the mission of security management and the strategic planning of its client. For this to fully reach fruition, the organization conducting the risk assessment must carefully document its process and findings. There is far more to a security risk assessment than just determining the likelihood, opportunity, and impact of its foreseeable risk. Every security program and its strategies are vulnerable to second guessing. What should this documentation include?

- A risk assessment policy and procedures should be prepared that is a separately indexed item in the Standing Operations Procedure (SOP) of the corporate security department or the operating department overseeing the asset protection process.
- The SOP should delineate the following:
  - The frequency of assessments. This could involve various frequencies or different strategies, depending upon the facility and its security needs. There is no "right" frequency or methodology. But the choices documented should be supported by internal or external consultation in response to the initial facility risk assessment.
  - The methodology (modalities) to be used in conducting the assessment must be based upon its capability to reasonably identify foreseeable risks. Once again, the choice should be supported by internal or external consultation in response to the initial facility's initial risk assessment.
- Documentation of risk assessments must link the identified risks with defensive strategies. Remember, your assessment is susceptible to after-the-act review. To avoid culpability each time a risk is identified (particularly after a security incident), the assessment should also discuss the alternate strategies that will be developed to deter, detect, deny, delay, respond to, and/or recover from the risk. Periodic

changes to strategy should always include a risk assessment prior to the strategy being upgraded and the rationale for the change. Constantly changing strategy (technological or procedural) without documenting *why* is a plan for failure and an easy target to criticism.

- Each time a system-wide or individual assessment is conducted, a *diary* of the process should be prepared. This "show and tell" is critical to demonstrating your organization's willingness to be aware of its security vulnerabilities, but also that you were responsive to the changes in your environment and business operations.

- Each organization is different. This documentation may appear to overburden valuable staff time. In small organizations this may be no more than a filed memo. But if your organization is subject to serious risk exposures, a risk assessment and responsive defensive strategy process will reap significant rewards if and when that foreseeable and high-impact risk does occur. Think of the time and energy your organization has taken with its crisis management, disaster recovery, or emergency evacuation procedures as examples. Would you want a major fire or other natural disaster without this crisis response plan?

- Risk assessments are not normally an add-on to the cost of managing a security operation. In fact, they should improve an organization's bottom line. Properly done, they will identify the responsive level of defensive strategy that is intrinsically needed; not what the vendor wants to sell you or the knee jerk reaction of management's response to an event. A professional security vendor (e.g. security officer service, technology management sales, etc.) should advise your organization to perform a risk assessment *before* they offer their products or services. It is actually in their self interest. An organization that has identified their risks and has linked this to strategies they need is a *buyer*, not an insecure shopper. This is why documenting the link between the identified risk and defensive strategy is so relevant. It is also why *convergence* is strategic in assisting with the assessment. It identifies how the integration of all operating groups can mitigate or eliminate duplicate costs in providing security strategies.

## CHAPTER TWO

The Nature of Risk

The types of foreseeable risk, their likelihood and opportunity to occur, and their impact to your organization's assets can never be taken for granted. A security risk assessment should become part of senior management and staff management's day-to-day stewardship of asset protection. The implementation of security risk assessment should not be a once-a-year process, but must be a day-to-day stewardship of an organization's multi-departmental operations with data input occurring from each on a timely basis. The discussions that follow are intended to highlight more frequently occurring risks from an historical perspective and how a security risk assessment is likely to prevent their occurrence. The exclusion of any risk does not infer that other risks are not equally relevant or a potential within your organization. It is also important to note that some high-technology industries and government facilities have significantly more complex risks that this text and its suggestions may not cover. However, much can be gained by following the outline presented in a high-risk environment. *All* risk occurrence can be mitigated by being identified and responsively managed. Risk assessment not only reveals the potential for security risks before the fact, but can also be used to understand the degree to which an ongoing or suspected threat has the potential to get out of control. The link between risk assessment and investigation can be blurred. An experienced investigator may be seeking a resolution to an ongoing loss, but by lacking sufficient risk assessment skills (or lacking the operational benefit of risk assessment) will succeed in securing a resolution of the who, what, when, where, and how of one event, but fail to identify what other loss potentials exist and what should be done in the future.

All incidents listed below use altered identification to protect the privacy of individuals and organizations.

Premises Liability

CASE #1 - CASINO

On a clear Sunday morning, John Farrell, from his tenth floor high-rise apartment, was staring out his patio window in the direction of an indoor parking garage abutting a well known hotel and casino. John noticed a young man sitting on the parapet of the roof of an indoor parking garage, seven stories up. He was sitting with his hands alongside his body, palms facing down. His legs were dangling over the edge of the parapet. John did not know how long he had been sitting there. He appeared to be nervously looking from side to side. John was a paramedic and intuitively believed that the man sitting on the roof was in trouble and might very well be a "jumper." He picked up the phone and called the casino security office to inform them of what he saw and what he thought might happen. Several minutes later John observed a security vehicle enter the roof parking level. Once the marked security patrol vehicle emerged up the ramp and on to the roof parking level it stopped. The vehicle did not appear to be going at a high rate of speed. No lights were flashing. The uniformed security officer got out of the patrol vehicle, looked over to the man sitting on the parapet, and appeared to be yelling something to him. The security officer was estimated to be approximately 50 feet away from the "jumper." All of these observations were seen by the witness from several blocks away, but there were no other witnesses. There was nothing unusual in the gestures of the security officer, nor did he make any attempt to move closer to the "jumper." The young man sitting on the parapet turned around, looked back at the security officer, then pressed down with his palms and slowly slid off the parapet plunging seven floors to his death. Discovery and investigation revealed that there were no physical deterrent on the roof's parapet to prevent someone from climbing on to, sitting, or jumping from the parapet. It was also established that the responding officer had never been trained in crisis resolution, particularly what the response should be in response to a potential suicide. Investigation further revealed in the after-the-fact discovery of this incident that there were three other suicides, all involving a "jumper" from other roof tops at other casinos in the area. These occurred in a two year period prior to the subject incident.

CASE #2 - RETAIL

Millie and Harold Rutledge took their children to the grand opening of a retail store at a nearby shopping center. They lived in a small town. The opening was a big event. One of the events scheduled for that day was a "dollar toss." The event was advertised for days on a local radio station, newspapers and in the shopping center. Representatives of the store went up on their roof (one story structure). A large crowd formed below. The idea was for the store to empty a large sack of dollar bills into the air. The breeze would gently carry and flutter the bills down into the crowd. The excited crowd would jump up and grasp for the dollars as fast as they could. This had always been an exciting, fun-filled and successful opening event. The breeze would often be so strong at prior events that promoters learned to attach a large paper clip to each bill to assure that they would not flutter too far from their intended audience. There had never been a serious problem at similar opening events held throughout the state. Harold and Millie Rutledge had arrived early with their children and wanted to be as close to the store as possible. It was their opinion that closer was better, with gravity serving as their friend. They were unfortunately right. On the day of this event there was a total calm. There was no breeze. When the sack of dollar bills was emptied, all of the bills, weighted with clips, fell in a vertical drop landing near the store's foundation. There was a crowd "surge" toward where the dollars dropped. There was no way Millie or Harold could get out of the way or hold back the crowd that was pressing against them in their excitement to get at the bills. One of their children was crushed to death; the other suffered multiple fractures. Millie and Harold's lives were forever destroyed. No risk assessment had ever been done for potential risks for this event; consequently no special crowd control strategies had been arranged.

CASE #3 - HEALTHCARE

Herman Smith was an individual residing at Pleasant View Commons in Dream, PA. Always Care Corporation operated Pleasant View Commons and was the corporate entity licensed in the State of Maine to do business as a personal care home. On 1/4/01, Herman Smith and Elaine Jones, executrix of the Smith estate, entered into an admission agreement with Pleasant View. They agreed to pay $1,450 per month in return for Mr. Smith's safety and comfort. In the early morning hours of 2/23/01, Helen Bennett and/or Zena Brown, personal care assistants at the subject location, disarmed the alarms at the facility. At 4:30 a.m., Mr. John Fennelly, while dropping off his mother at work at Joyful Manor, an assisted care facility across the street from the subject location, discovered Herman Smith in only his underwear lying in the rear parking lot driveway. The temperature outside was below freezing. Mr. Fennelly went to the open loading dock door of Pleasant View and freely walked through the hallways and encountered Ms. Bennett and Ms. Brown (personal care assistants) to advise them of the man outside. The personal care assistants went outside, looked at Mr. Smith and stated that he was *not* one of their residents (it was later verified that Mr. Smith *was* a resident). The police were then called and arrived at the scene at 4:41 a.m. Mr. Smith was taken to the hospital where he later died of hypothermia. Investigation of this incident revealed that both personal assistants had criminal conviction backgrounds. On the evening of the subject incident, both had gone out for personal reasons which violated Pleasant View's procedures. In doing so, they left the perimeter alarm system off and never re-armed it upon returning, allowing Mr. Smith to elope without detection.

CASE #4 - OFFICE BUILDING

Harry Ming was a security officer employed with Always Secure Security. They were contracted by Safe Insurance Company in their corporate office building in Serene, IL. Mr. Ming was hired by Always Safe and instructed to provide access control to the main lobby of Serene's office building. Hours for security officer services were evenings after 6:00 p.m. until 6:00 a.m. and throughout weekends and holidays. Security officers assigned to Safe's building were specifically instructed *not* to leave the lobby area and additionally advised that no upper floors could be visited. Restroom facilities existed in the lobby and the officers were to lock the front door should they need to use the restroom. Meals brought in by the officers were to be consumed at their lobby post. On March 18, 1990, Mr. Ming locked the front door, left his post, and went to the fourth floor of the office building where Safe's homeowners insurance files for their clients were located. Mr. Ming went through the client files looking for those involving insurance coverage (riders) for jewelry. He noted which properties did or did not have alarm systems. Some contained drawings of the perimeter and interior of the homes. He made copies from the files of home inventories (jewelry, etc.), addresses, and names of those residing in the properties. On May 20, 1990, Mr. Ming broke into the residence of one of Serene's clients at approximately 3:00 a.m. Residing in the property were Mrs. Foster and her 14 year old daughter Julie who were at home when Mr. Ming entered the property. He awakened both women and demanded to know where the jewelry and cash were located. After their safe was opened, he secured both women with strong duct tape placing each in separate rooms. He sexually assaulted both women before removing the jewelry and cash from the safe. Later discovery and investigation determined that Mr. Ming had an extensive criminal background that had not been detected. Discovery also developed that inspections of the security officers were not being conducted as contracted and that none had occurred on the evening of the subject incident. No other measures were taken to ensure that the officer was at his assigned post. Access to the elevators was unrestricted, without an access control system to authorize and monitor elevator use in the evening. The offices and file cabinets for Safe Insurance were also not secured.

CASE # 5 - EVENT

Mary Oscalli was attending a motorcycle racing event in a popular mountain resort. The event had been held each summer for years and was always scheduled over the Fourth of July weekend. The land was leased to a promoter who used the winter-time ski area for biking enthusiasts. Racers from all over the state gathered for this event. Food and beer were served as local musicians entertained the fans. Attendees, between races, would lay out on the lawn and picnic. As the day wore on and beer continued to be consumed, it became a dominant factor in the festive mood of the crowd. Besides the festive atmosphere, some grew irritable and a few disagreements flared up. Security officers assigned to the event were trained to quickly isolate and contain these problems. Off-duty police officers were also deployed. Throughout the event attendees could hear firecrackers going off. Attendees at the event brought these fireworks to the event. The event promoters and operators did not provide the fireworks entertainment and were not licensed or authorized by township officials to do so. On occasion, loud explosions were heard. The concussion from these devices could be felt some distance away. Those detonating the devices usually moved away from the crowd when they lit the fuse and tossed it in a safe direction. They were "cherry bombs." Some were larger devices. Everyone knew this happened each year; so did police and security. It was part of the event and its past. After all, this was a "bikers" crowd. What's the problem! Neither the promoter, the police, or its security officer service had anything to do with overseeing, sanctioning, or providing the fireworks. Some teenagers, who were able to purchase and/or consume beer and who were tossing the cherry bombs decided to have some fun and tossed one in the direction of a crowd of other teenagers they knew. The device deflected off a tree and landed directly alongside Mary Oscalli and her preteen children sitting on a blanket. When she saw this device land within inches of one of her children, she instinctively reached for the device to throw it out of harm's way. The device detonated in her hand. Mary lost three fingers. Her son suffered a hearing loss and both suffered post traumatic anxiety neurosis arising from this incident.

CASE #6 - MANUFACTURING

On Sunday, January 18, 1995, the refrigeration units at Heavy Manufacturing, a wholly owned subsidiary of a multi-national corporation, in Heaven, NY, was vandalized and copper piping was stolen from the roof. Two companies were called in to make repairs on the property by Freezing Refrigeration and Lucky Seven Contractors. On Tuesday, January 27, 1995, one week later, a fire started on the northwest corner of the roof at a point approximately 50 feet from the northwest wall and 40 feet from the southwest wall in a heating/cooling unit. The fire extended to the electrical panel of the unit and to the gas supply piping beneath the unit. Fire also extended to rubberized roofing membrane in the area of the unit. It further extended, driven by strong gusty winds to similar roofing materials and was driven by the wind in a southeasterly direction across the surface of the roof. The fire further extended, probably by a drop down of molten roofing materials to the interior and contents of an occupancy in the southeast corner with bales of clothing and rags. The fire was extinguished by the Heaven Fire Department. The building was declared a total loss. The fire department investigation concluded that there was evidence of vandals being on the roof on the night of the fire. The fire investigation also concluded that arson was the cause of the fire. It should be noted that the investigation also revealed that Heavy Manufacturing had a persistent history of youths from the surrounding community being on the roof as well as vandalizing the perimeter of the property.

CASE #7 - HOTEL

On Saturday, March 20, 2004, George Miller, decedent, was attending a party being held at the Happy Hotel located in Best Town, KY. The party was held in two adjoining guest rooms. The party was attended by approximately 40 high school students. The rooms were rented to 19 year old Alecia Smith who arrived on the premises at approximately 6:00 p.m. with some friends and brought food and soft drinks into the rooms in preparation for the party. Guests to the party began arriving at about 9:00 p.m. George Miller was a guest of Ms. Smith. The party was extremely loud and hotel guests complained. Security visited the rooms and asked the party goers to be quiet. Evidence later concluded that during the security person's visit and subsequent visits, the hotel had actual notice that the guest rooms were being used for a teenage party. The police were never called, nor was Alecia Smith asked to end the party and ask her guests to leave. Some of the guests were clearly under the age of 21 and were intoxicated. It was not known where the alcoholic beverages came from. A loud argument spilled into the hallway between certain guests and one of the guests had a gun. This guest, during an altercation, discharged the handgun through the door whereupon George Miller was struck by two bullets resulting in his death. Alice Johnson was also shot in the head but survived and is blind in her left eye.

CASE #8 - LIGHT INDUSTRIAL

John Russell was on medical leave from his employer of over 25 years. He was permitted to retain his photo i.d. and visit the plant to use the cafeteria and other company resources. He had been on medical leave for almost two years. Mr. Russell's medical problem was determined to be related to environment issues with his employment. He was being treated and his medical expenses were covered by the company health plan. While this was in process, the company was sold to an investor who made it clear to Mr. Russell and others that medical treatment and benefits would be discontinued in the near future. Mr. Russell became embittered and on his next visit to the cafeteria showed his friends a 9mm pistol. He held it up in the air and distinctly stated that certain executives now in the firm were going to see the "other end" of his weapon. Employees did not take Mr. Russell seriously, but they did report it to the security department. Mr. Russell was observed being dressed in camouflage clothing with a Soldier of Fortune magazine stuffed in his back pocket when the manager of security stopped by to see him and instruct him not to bring the gun into the plant again. He was ***not*** banned from returning to the plant. His house was filled with other military memorabilia that included an extensive weapons collection that he was proud to show off. The next week Mr. Russell returned to the cafeteria. He did not bring a gun. This time he had in his hands a bag containing a model airplane, gas operated, that could actually be flown. Taped to the fuselage of the model plane were two sticks of dynamite. He told his friends that he was going to fly the model plane over the executive offices of the plant and crash it into the offices. Once again his friends thought this to be quite humorous and did not take him seriously, but security was again contacted. In ***neither*** case did security report the incidents to senior management or human resources. Discovery later determined that the Manager of Security took it upon himself to keep an eye on Mr. Russell when he came to the plant. Mr. Russell visited the plant one more time dressed in a rain coat. The security manager did not note his arrival. Under this coat he concealed an AK47 automatic weapon. Later it was learned that he also had a concealed, 9mm pistol, 300 rounds of ammunition, and a list of 60 names that he intended to "terminate" (learned from a note found in his pocket). He entered the plant through the entrance leading to the executive offices, walked up the stairs to the receptionist (who had not been advised by security to alert them if Mr. Russell visited). Mr. Russell immediately shot the receptionist who later died. He then calmly walked down the executive corridor firing his weapon at different executives. In the process of shooting 22 persons, eight were killed. Mr. Russell then took his own life with his 9mm pistol when cornered by local police. Considerably more employees would have been shot and killed had it not been for the heroic effort of a security officer (stationed at the main gate outside and unarmed) who surreptitiously followed Mr. Russell. This officer maintained communication with the police using his cell phone and identified Mr. Russell's location when they arrived.

CASE #9 - HIGH SCHOOL

On April 4, 2002, John Connelly was a freshman at the Smart Valley High School in North Pole, AK. At approximately 7:15 a.m. on the above noted date, Mr. Connelly entered the school for the first time that school day through the side entrance. He was driven to school by his mother. He was dropped off less than 20 yards from the side entrance to the school. Shortly after he entered the school, he was savagely sat upon, punched, kicked, held down, and beaten by anywhere from six to 10 assailants. It was alleged that some and/or all of the assailants had been drinking alcohol and/or had consumed illicit drugs on the morning of the attack. The assailants were under the influence of such intoxicants when they entered the school to search for and assault John Connelly. All assailants who assaulted Mr. Connelly were dressed similarly in black clothing and were acting in a gang-like manner. Mr. Connelly's assault lasted approximately five to 10 minutes and took place both inside the school and on the concrete steps located directly outside the school's door. During this time, there was no intervention by school officials or employees, security personnel, or any other agent of the school. The local police were not called until after the incident. Mr. Connelly further testified that some of the assailants were students at the school and some were not. This type of event had persistently occurred during the school year. Mr. Connelly's injuries were significant and involved life-long physical disabilities.

SUMMARY OF CASE STUDIES

- In each of the above, the defendants had not conducted any risk assessment prior to or during the planning of their event and/or security program.
- After-the-fact risk assessments convinced juries that each of the above security incidents were *reasonably foreseeable.*
- No security strategies had been developed that were responsive to the type of risk which occurred in the subject incidents.
- The failure by defendants to conduct sufficient analysis of their potential security risks and provide responsive security strategies was determined, in each case, to be a significant producing cause of the incidents.

All of these risks are different in that they do not represent the stereotypical description of a security risk (e.g., violence in the workplace, information theft, fraud, robbery, sexual assault, etc.). Nevertheless, the victims of each and/or their families suffered from highly traumatic events which were proven to be predictable and preventable. In each case, the property owners and/or operators were defendants in civil actions and ended up being directly or indirectly responsible for substantial civil awards to the plaintiffs. In each case the negative impact to their reputation was significant. The following threats are more commonly understood to be potentially significant to an organization.

Event Risk Issues

In discussing the mitigation of civil liability with event management, an interesting phrase from the Web site of Diversified Management Services, "Strategic Planning Services" states, "If you don't know where you're going, any road will take you there." This, of course, applies to ending up in court defending against an action that alleges inadequate security where a spectator or other "business invitee" is injured after a "foreseeable" security and safety incident. We all know that getting there, no matter how well-planned the security program is, can often be unavoidable as we never can "guarantee" that every spectator or patron will not become injured while being a patron at a bar, sporting event, concert, etc.

A consultant was once asked by an event planner to provide a security program for a special event soon to be held at their new city-owned stadium. He was interested in permanent as well as temporary changes (technological and procedural), but needed an operational guideline and budget as soon as possible to deal with the upcoming special event (major rock concert). The event had been planned as a public relations venue to attract the community to the new stadium. When the consultant asked what he was trying to prevent or manage, he looked at the consultant, eyebrows raised and shoulders shrugged, and stated, "You know what happens!" At that moment the client must have sincerely believed that he was wasting his time with that consultant. Many minutes of discussion later, he was convinced that a *risk assessment* by his security personnel with other stadium staff and public law enforcement before each and every event was mandatory. The consultant agreed with him that there were basic procedural and technological crowd control tactics for any event at the new stadium, but if he wasn't prepared to routinely conduct a risk assessment to identify unique security risks *prior to each* event held at the stadium, he would be in for some very unpleasant surprises implementing a "basic vanilla" security program, and he would not have been able to respond to and/or manage anomalous and violent events.

"An understanding of the meaning of "risk factor" was an underlying question for many of those who participated in the survey. First of all, a "risk factor" is one that identifies something that is an actual possibility of injury, death, property damage, damage to public image, claims and lawsuits. In business it always boils down to money but some losses cannot be adequately computed to a monetary value. There are other terms that are often used that directly relate to what is generically defined as a risk factor including perils, hazards, threats, and vulnerabilities...

In addition, risk factors include the concerns of the various entities involved in the event. These concerns may or may not be accurate or verifiable but must be addressed since the actions, decisions and allocations made by these individuals is based on their concerns. Whether the concerns are phobic or unlikely, they must still be identified and evaluated..." [12]

Special information, can be provided to assist with the nature of a particular event. Reference can be made to "The Rock Safety Database™" developed by Crowd

12. *Special Event Security Management, Loss Prevention and Emergency Service,* Chapter 2, pp., 11-12, Alexander Berlonghi, M.S., Bookmasters, Inc., 1996.

Management Strategies.[13] This database enables an evaluator to learn if a band has a history of concert trouble before it plays your town. If you're involved in concert public safety, the Rock Safety Database™ (RSD) will help you plan more effectively and, if necessary, help provide backup data you need to justify additional safety precautions, staffing, or equipment. The database covers crowd safety problems and issues from 1952 to the present and is continuously updated using a multitude of sources. Similar databases are available in other venues (i.e. sports) as well. It is a powerful planning tool with a reputation for accuracy. The client was also introduced to two other techniques (e.g., benchmarking, inherent risk analysis, etc.) where like venues throughout the country are surveyed to determine risks.

This discussion does not inclusively identify all strategies; that list would be entirely too long to discuss. The purpose is to impress upon the reader where they may be *after* a major incident and how they will be perceived in court or in the realm of public opinion. There is no such thing as a vanilla security program. Your program must be driven by data and that data must be directed by risk assessment. As we stated from the onset, any road may take you there, but be certain you will be comfortable and secure at your destination!

VIOLENCE IN THE WORKPLACE

A consultant received a phone call from one of his clients that a very serious and potentially dangerous threat had been made by one of their employees to his supervisor. The person making the threat felt victimized by his supervisor over a period of time and "planned to get even." The client told the consultant that they intended to immediately terminate the employee and wanted advice as to what security steps should be taken when they did. The termination was planned for that same day. A discussion with the client determined that the threat was, in fact, quite serious. After a long discussion, the consultant convinced the client *not* to immediately terminate the employee as this would only serve to additionally victimize him and exacerbate an already potentially explosive circumstance. If an immediate termination occurred, it was considered predicable that the threatening employee would return to the plant or go to his supervisor's home and act out his threat placing many other persons at risk as well. An immediate (same day) arrangement was made for the threatening employee to be interviewed with law enforcement standing by in an adjoining office. An arrangement was also made to provide security for the threatened employee and his family until a resolution could be made. The threatening employee agreed to security performing a "pat down" to ensure

---

13. www.crowdsafe.com

that no weapon was on his person before the interview took place. Those interviewing the employee included a security and human resource representative. The interview resulted in the employee agreeing to a temporary suspension for violating company rules for making threats to his supervisor and further agreeing to participate in an employee assistance program for the evaluation and remedial response to his stress. The long term result with the threatening employee was him agreeing to a permanent severance, and assistance with job replacement services to seek alternate employment. This response to the threat of violence prevented additional victimization to the distressed employee and the protection of the person threatened.

Violent Incident Investigation

The tracking of incident data, no matter how well implemented, cannot serve as the only strategy that an organization needs in assessing violence in the workplace and responding with an adequate security program. Incident data may provide insights to future events, but more than likely serves to corroborate existing or anomalous conditions causing violence and should not be the sole basis for policy and procedures. In this regard :

- Each and every violent incident or threat occurring in your organization should be reported to appropriate channels and investigated immediately. It is entirely insufficient to use the summary of prior statistics rather than an analysis of what actually occurred. The investigation of each violent incident should identify:

- Date, time, and day of week?

- Specific location of incident?

- Type of weapon, if any, used?

- Were drugs involved? Alcohol?

- Full statement from all witness for each incident to identify the how, what, when, where, and why the incident occurred.

- What remedial action is taken when your organization first becomes aware of a potential violent person or event? Does your program integrate with Human Resources and senior management?

- What remedial action is taken after each event?

- An analysis of the effectiveness of each procedural and physical security strategy that was in place prior to and in response to the event. This should be done after all violent events.

This will assist your risk assessment department in determining the degree to which your organization is prepared for violence in the workplace. The better the program is in preventing and responding to violence in the workplace, the less likely a repeat incident will occur.

TERRORISM

For terrorist threats, the attractiveness of the facility as a target is a primary consideration. In addition, the type of terrorist act may vary based on the potential adversary and the method of attack most likely to be successful for a given scenario. For example, a terrorist wishing to strike against the federal government may be more likely to attack a large federal building than to attack a multi-tenant office building containing a large number of commercial tenants and a few government tenants. However, if security at the large federal building makes mounting a successful attack too difficult, the terrorist may be diverted to a nearby facility that may not be as attractive from an occupancy perspective, but has a higher probability of success due to the absence of adequate security. In general, the likelihood of terrorist attacks cannot be quantified statistically since terrorism is, by its very nature, random. Hence, when considering terrorist threats, the concept of developing credible threat packages is important. Knowledge is the essential first step to careful threat assessment and planning, which enable law enforcement decision makers to build a comprehensive and effective counter-terrorism strategy. The agencies, organizations, and resources listed in the below noted Web site specialize in counter-terrorism and security expertise with the following subject matter:

- Border Security & Immigration
- Critical Infrastructure
- Cyberterrorism
- Domestic Security
- Equipment & Communications
- First Responders
- International Security
- Medical & Public Health Issues
- Threat Assessment
- Transportation Security

- Weapons of Mass Destruction.[14]

Uncertainty in terrorism risk estimates suggests the need to devise means of hedging our homeland security policies against a range of distributions of risk that are plausible given what we know about uncertainties in our risk estimation procedures. So, rather than seek an optimal method for estimating risk, we seek a method that leads us to make the least egregious errors in decision making across the range of possible scenarios that might develop in the future. This presents a problem comparable to that of forecasting economic trends using multiple estimates or models discussed by Clemen (1989). This literature highlights two objectives to consider when combining estimates: 1) use information contained in the multiple estimates to improve forecasting accuracy; and 2) make note of and retain the important distinctions that individual estimates represent. Addressing multiple values or objectives in terrorism risk estimates differs from combining forecasts. While the goal of combining forecasts is to develop an accurate estimate, the goal of considering multiple objectives is to reflect appropriately the range of values held by stakeholders. Literature on multi-objective decision making provides several approaches for addressing the fact that terrorism risk can be expressed in multiple outcomes. The commonality across these methods is the need to reflect transparently a range of values for multiple objectives in the decision making process.

Simple Versus Complex Risk Indicators

Despite the many sources of uncertainty surrounding terrorism risk, estimating this risk is necessary for informed distribution of homeland security resources. Approaches that have been used in policy analysis for estimating terrorism risk are bounded by two generic categories: simple risk indicators and event-based models. Each approach reflects the components of terrorism risk.[15]

Quantitative Terrorism Risk Assessment

The task of quantifying terrorism risk should not be confused with predicting the next terrorist attack. This important distinction between risk assessment and event prediction exists also with natural perils. No seismologist is capable of predicting the time, place and magnitude of the next major earthquake in California, but it is possible for a seismic risk analyst to evaluate the annual accedence probability of loss to a California property portfolio. Large earthquakes are impossible to predict because of a haphazard random element in the manner in which the rupture of a geological fault

---

14. *Rand Corporation: http://www.rand.org/pubs/monographs/2005/RAND_MG388.pdf*
15. *http://www.rand.org/pubs/monographs/2005/RAND_MG388.pdf*

propagates and eventually stops. This randomness contributes to the so called aleatory uncertainty in earthquake occurrence (Woo [1999]), which is readily accounted for within a probabilistic risk assessment, but confounds attempts at deterministic event prediction. This distinction between risk assessment and event prediction matters to civic authorities and insurers. Being responsible primarily for public safety, civic authorities would ideally like to have reliable predictions to warn against imminent hazard events, or prioritize urgent defensive measures (Cordesman [2002]). Insurers, on the other hand, seek to quantify risk not over a brief time window of a few days, but spread over a number of months. [16]

Summary of Terrorism Threats

The degree to which an organization should consider a responsive security program for the threat of terrorism is as varied as the number of facilities that potentially could be victimized. Once an organization has taken reasonable steps to evaluate their potential for a terroristic attack, the response could be to do nothing, or at a minimum train security and other organizational staff to be aware of persons paying unusual attention (conducting surveillance) of their facility (which could include photography). Where the risk potential from well-defined resources identifies the threat to be more serious and likely, the response could vary from well trained and possibly armed security officer patrol, high impact barriers and/or other sophisticated technological surveillance systems. The investment in these strategies is, of course, a highly subjective decision that can only be clarified by a well-defined risk assessment program and the reality of current political circumstances. In each instance, however, the crisis response and disaster recovery policy and procedures (including all necessary integration with public safety resources) must be considered. Loss mitigation in response and recovery may be the only viable option to certain predictable terror events.

IT SECURITY

Historical Perspective

In the 1950s through the 1970s security management was a discipline that primarily provided asset protection though mechanical hardware—not solid state technology. Security officer services and investigative services were the stalwarts of most defensive strategies. Alarm companies in the 50s and 60s were still installing "trip wires" from wall to wall with clips at the end of the trip wire plugged into electrical contacts. The advent of solid state technology started with alarm control panels and detection sensors

---

16. *Quantitative Terrorism Risk Assessment,* Dr. Gordon Foo, Risk Management Solutions, Ltd.
http://www.weatherdesk.net/NewsPress/Quantitative_Terrorism_Risk_Assessment.pdf

that had integrated circuits which could intelligently operate/monitor the devices they "interactively communicated with." Computers inched their way into information based technology slowly and at first cumbersomely. In 1970 a central station alarm company installed the first computerized integration with incoming alarm signals from direct wire, multiplex, and digital dial-up transmitters. This computer actually was two as a full second was required with a physical switch known as a "knife" switch for moving to the back-up CPU in case of system failure to the primary. The room which contained these computers was approximately 20' x 17'. The system produced so much heat from its vacuum tubes that the air from the room was evacuated to the outside by fans and air conditioning was an essential. Twenty years later the same system could have been totally replaced and vastly improved in operating efficiently with an inexpensive laptop adding room for significant growth and integrity.

The above perspective is offered to move the reader's awareness to just how quickly the security industry and its clients have moved from mechanical use to complete reliance upon modern micro-state functioning and information storage capacity. Today there is literally no significant limitation on the ability of business to rely upon hugely powerful operating and storage capacities. In just two decades, business threats leaped to an entirely different threat potential that, in a worse case scenario, could be life threatening to an organization. Consequently the security management industry has had little time to adjust their knowledge and operating experience base to deal with this threat. The reaction to this reality was a very slow assimilation of informational asset protection with security management practitioners and public law enforcement. This assimilation is still a work-in-progress. The vacuum resulting from the immediate need for information security came primarily from IT practitioners who understood the esoteric threats and could initiate the process of asset management to information, computer hardware, software, networks, and telecommunications. This has led to the current professional designation of a "CSO (Computer Security Officer)" in corporate America. But the protection of information-based assets required more than esoteric knowledge and experience. The objective of information-based security also required the management of *people* who often were the root cause of the problems and were not part of the solution. Personnel security, investigations, and the physical and procedural security to facilities housing information and IT technology were some of the objectives that few IT Security Managers had adequate experience with. It was therefore strategic that the *convergence* of the CSO and others in IT with Security Management and others having the stewardship for asset protection be implemented. This is discussed in Chapter 3 (Convergence as it applies to Risk Assessment). This has been slow to happen in many organization due to a well known obstacle "turf wars." As IT managers developed staff and operating efficiencies they were slow to accept Security Management and other corporate staff into their process. They were concerned that this integratioh may convolute their efficiencies and decrease the effectiveness of their IT Security program. Conversely, Security Management staff were equally slow to accept those from security management or other staff positions having the stewardship of other asset protection for similar reasons.

Purpose of Risk Management (In IT Security)

All business decisions, in IT or otherwise, are an exercise in the evaluation of the risk of inaction versus the cost of action to reduce risks (real or perceived). Risk Management is helpful in answering questions such as whether failing to upgrade your file-and-print server will affect the ability of users to do their jobs properly; whether implementation of the latest intrusion detection technology will reduce the likelihood of someone breaking into your email server; and whether a firewall is necessary to protect your Web server, or if simple router ACLs (access control lists) will suffice. Furthermore, a risk management process will help you prioritize these issues should you lack the resources necessary to address them all immediately.

In today's hyper-competitive world, the use of risk management is vital to the long-term success of your company. Not all risks can be eliminated: the cost in resources and time would be prohibitive. In fact, most businesses need to take some risks to gain a competitive edge. Therefore, you must decide when and where educated risks can be taken and how finite resources should be allocated to reduce risk and support business strategies.

Risk management enables sound judgment when taking risks, and affords a level of contingency planning should a risk become a reality. Understanding the risks to company assets is the starting point of a risk management process. Once you understand the risks to your business, you'll be able to make sound decisions on whether to accept, mitigate or transfer those risks. In addition, risk management pulls together data from other security areas, such as vulnerability analysis and operations monitoring, to provide an overall view of business risk. The focus of this discussion is the application of techniques for risk management and risk assessment to modern information security practices.

Risk Management in a Nutshell

Risk management can be loosely defined as a systematic process for the identification, analysis, control and communication of risks. In the business world, these risks may vary from the mundane (the risk of an accounting error, for example) to the esoteric (say, the risk of a cracker taking advantage of a little-known application bug). Risk management should be integrated into the life cycle of any process or project that's important to a business. The use of a risk management methodology lets a company make informed decisions about the allocation of scarce resources to areas that are the most at risk.

Risk management should be an ongoing activity that includes phases for assessing risk, implementing controls, promoting awareness, and monitoring effectiveness. At the heart of risk assessment which is the evaluation of the potential impact of threats on the ability of a company to continue providing products or services to customers. This evaluation phase of the process is risk assessment.

Risk Management, often confused with vulnerability assessment/analysis, which is a critical phase in any security risk assessment is widely used in both the public and private sectors to support decision-making processes. Employing risk assessment methodologies to drive decision-making processes around security and associated technology allows for consistent and effective use of decision-support data, as well as removal of technical bias from what are essentially business decisions.

Risk Assessment Process Overview

Risk assessment is a process for tying together information gathered about business assets, their value and their associated vulnerabilities, to produce a measure of the risk to the business from a given project, implementation or design.[17]

Challenges Associated With Assessing Information Security Risks

Reliably assessing information security risks can be more difficult than assessing other types of risks, because the data on the likelihood and costs associated with information security risk factors are often more limited and because risk factors are constantly changing. For example, data are limited on risk factors, such as the likelihood of a sophisticated hacker attack and the costs of damage, loss, or disruption caused by events that exploit security weaknesses; some costs, such as loss of customer confidence or disclosure of sensitive information, are inherently difficult to quantify; although the cost of the hardware and software needed to strengthen controls may be known, it is often not possible to precisely estimate the related indirect costs, such as the possible loss of productivity that may result when new controls are implemented.

This lack of reliable and current data often precludes precise determinations of which information security risks are the most significant and comparisons of which

---

17. *http://www.networkcomputing.com/1121/1121f3.html*

controls are the most cost-effective. Because of these limitations, it is important that organizations identify and employ methods that efficiently achieve the benefits of risk assessment while avoiding costly attempts to develop seemingly precise results that are of questionable reliability.

Involve Business and Technical Experts

Drawing on knowledge and expertise from a wide range of sources was viewed as essential to help ensure that all important risk factors were considered. Managers generally had the best understanding of the criticality and sensitivity of individual business operations and of the systems and data that supported these operations. Accordingly, they were usually in the best position to gauge the business impact of system misuse or disruption. Conversely, technical personnel, including security specialists, brought to the process an understanding of existing system designs and vulnerabilities and of the potential benefits, costs, and performance impacts associated with new controls being considered. As a result, meetings conducted during the risk assessment process usually included a variety of individuals from the business unit with expertise in business operations and processes, security, information resource management, information technology, and system operations. Others from outside the business unit might also be included, such as internal auditors and, occasionally, contractors with specific pertinent expertise. All the organizations relied almost exclusively on in-house personnel to perform the risk assessment rather than contractors. The computer hardware and software company initially relied on contractors to assist in conducting assessments but eventually determined that relying on contractors deprived its own personnel of valuable experience in exploring risk.

Hold Business Units Responsible

Responsibility for initiating and conducting risk assessments, as well as following up on resulting recommendations, lay primarily with the individual business units. Business units were considered to be in the best position to determine when an assessment was needed and to ensure that recommendations for risk reduction techniques resulting from the assessment were implemented effectively. At the financial services company, the business units annually developed risk management plans from a variety of information sources, including the results of prior risk assessments. These plans served as a basis for establishing priorities for performing risk assessments; designating individuals to facilitate, coordinate, and execute risk assessment activities; and determining the tolerable level of risk for a given operation. At the computer hardware and software company, business unit managers were responsible for assessing the risks associated with their unit's computer-based operations, and such responsibilities were generally documented in their performance expectations.[18]

FRAUD

An enterprising college student, working in the data processing department of a major insurance organization, came up with a scheme for extra spending money. While working in the data center, he was able to download lists of persons being contacted by the insurance company's sales agents, which was data from all of the sales agents calling in who wanted actuarial life insurance estimates for quotations. The college student, working at night and under minimum supervision began selling these lists to competing insurance company salesmen. One of the sales agents contacted was keen enough to advise his employer of the scheme and the college student's venture was terminated.

In another event, a recent college graduate, James Smith, had just started as an accountant for a small grocery store chain when he realized that there was something definitely wrong with the books. Leasing expenses for the five stores seemed unusually high. Stranger still, the lease checks were made out to two companies even though there was only one landlord. When he searched for the canceled checks, he found nothing, yet the bank statements indicated that the checks had cleared. Smith phoned the landlord, who claimed he never billed the company. Now completely perplexed, this young accountant rushed to the bank for copies of the checks. He stared at the distinctive handwriting on their backs and realized, with a sick feeling, that it belonged to his predecessor. The former accountant had set up a bank account under a phony corporate name and siphoned about $75,000 over three years. For a retail operation whose fragile existence hinged on a steady cash flow, the loss could have buried the business.

Size of Problem

The above events and thousands more like them, smaller and significantly larger, are a daily occurrence in business operations. From low level hourly employees malfeasance to multi-million dollar salaried executives who have used their positions to feather their financial circumstances by millions, the frequency and impact of fraud risks have cost business billions. The ripple effect of these threats can be enormous to the economy, shareholders, and persons who are dependent upon the financial well being of the organization. Current major corporate fraud has included abuse with

18. http://www.gao.gov/special.pubs/ai00033.pdf

stock option configurations and the pirating of employee pension funds. It is not only what fraud can be occasioned to the organization, but what fraud can be perpetrated upon the public *by* the organization. There appears to be no limit to the frequency of serious business fraud. Because of the unique position of insiders and contractors, all fraud cannot be prevented. But responsive measures can be taken to mitigate the likelihood, impact, and response to such risks. One way (by far not the only) is to have an competent understanding in advance of what fraud risk potentials do exist resulting from your organization's unique business operations, its accounting practices, and the degree to which sub-contracted accounting services are free to exercise audit and remedial measure to prevent fraud.

Entity-Level Fraud Risk Assessment Process

The Sarbanes-Oxley Act (SOX) of 2002 requires public companies, among other things, to evaluate the sufficiency of controls in place to prevent and detect fraud within the organization. Specific to fraud, Section 404 of SOX requires that each company have a documented and on-going process to identify, assess, and evaluate fraud risks related to internal control over financial reporting (fraud risks). Section 404 also clearly directs responsibility for the establishment and monitoring of such a process to Company Management and the Company's Board of Directors and Audit Committee.

Risk Assessment Scope

In order to clearly define the scope of this risk assessment, the definition of key terms utilized throughout the course of this exercise are provided below:

ABC Company defines fraud as any intentional act that is committed to secure an unfair or unlawful gain. The four categories of fraud related to internal control over financial reporting considered by management in this assessment are:

- Fraudulent Financial Reporting. Most fraudulent financial reporting schemes involve earnings management arising from improper revenue recognition, and overstatement of assets or understatement of liabilities.
- Misappropriation of Assets This category involves external and internal schemes, such as embezzlement, payroll fraud, and theft.
- Expenditures and liabilities for improper purposes This category refers to commercial and public bribery, as well as other improper payment schemes.
- Fraudulently obtained revenue and assets, costs and expense avoided. This category refers to schemes where an entity commits a fraud against its employees or third

parties, or when an entity improperly avoids an expense, such as tax fraud.

Additionally, it is important to note that various fraud schemes/scenarios can be perpetuated at many different locations or levels within an organization. For the purpose of this assessment, ABC Company considers fraud that can occur at three levels:

- Account-level
- Process-level
- Entity-level

Account-level and process-level fraud risks are defined as risks that are contained to a specific account or process, and their impact does not have a significant impact to the organization as a whole. As such, these risks will be identified and evaluated as part of the process documentation created for each relevant business area. Within the control documentation for each business process, specific, relevant fraud risks will be identified, and corresponding controls will be linked to these risks and tested based upon their significance. Management defines entity-level fraud risks as those schemes and scenarios that may be undertaken by employees, agents, vendors, or other parties that could have a material impact to the organization, either directly through financial statement impact or through other indirect means (e.g., stock price decline, reputation deterioration, etc.). Entity-level fraud risks will be considered separately. Compliance Audit prepared a risk and control matrix of entity-level fraud risks and associated controls for the organization. The presentation of these risks and controls will be similar to the control documentation prepared for individual business processes. The remainder of this document details the process by which entity-level fraud risks were identified and assessed throughout the organization.[19]

CONCLUSION

The lists and types of business and risk/threat potentials are endless. Their presentation above was to orient the reader's awareness and understanding of the unique relationship between risk assessment and the prevention of risk. As stated in the introduction, the fact that anomalous events do occur should not excuse or rationalize failing to perform adequate planning. It is inevitable that all risks will not be identified, but the very fact that a capable risk assessment paradigm is part of an organization's day-to-day stewardship of asset protection puts the organization in a far more defensible posture. Colleagues may disagree as to the nature and degree of security strategies;

---

19. *Quantitative Terrorism Risk Assessment,* Dr. Gordon Foo, Risk Management Solutions, Ltd. *http://www.weatherdesk.net/NewsPress/Quantitative_Terrorism_Risk_Assessment.pdf*

this is why setting security "standards" is such a rocky road. However, *conducting a risk assessment prior to implementing or upgrading a security program should be a standard security practice (standard of care) to which all security professionals adhere*.

## CHAPTER THREE

Convergence as It Applies to Risk Assessment

INTRODUCTION

Merriam-Webster's Collegiate Dictionary defines "convergence" as "the act of converging and especially moving toward union or uniformity."

In January and March 1975, *Security World* (Cahners Publishing) published two articles (Part I and II), *The Security/Safety Merger*. This insightful article was written by Arthur E. Torrington, who, at the time the article was published was Director of Executive Security & Intelligence Services of St. James, New York, a Long Island based consulting firm dealing in loss prevention and investigative services.

"From earlier times, man has sought to protect himself from felonious acts of others—and in today's world we call that function "security." Man has also set up barriers to guard himself from the duncery of his own negligence—and we call that function "safety." Both are aimed at loss prevention. Yet until recently a sharp separation in safety and security activities marked the loss prevention field.

Security, such as it was, had traditionally received its greatest emphasis in retail enterprises and in defense industries; while safety, largely because of its exposure to losses arising out of workmen's compensation claims, had received primary attention from the insurance industry. Both fields, however, address themselves directly to the reduction of losses in order to augment the overall profit picture.

Today (1975), an increased awareness of the similarity in purpose that links safety and security has encouraged the development of loss prevention as a legitimate management function. Both safety and security are qualities, or conditions that are conducive to the establishment of a satisfactory work environment. Both directly affect morale, productivity, the integrity of operations, and the protection of organizational assets. An examination of these quickly demonstrates that loss prevention is exactly what it says it is—*a functional aspect of business management wherein all activity is aimed at the formulation and implementation of safety and security policies and programs specifically designed to prevent, reduce, or eliminate internal and external losses* (highlight and italics were included in the article)." [20]

Reading this article was akin to reading Life Magazine for the month and year of your birth date and reviewing with delight the advertisements of the time. Yet, in 1975, Mr. Torrington's article was amazingly prescient in so many ways. He foresaw the need for *convergence* between safety and security. Although "security management" was not yet part of his lexicon, neither were the threats of globalization, the International Jihad terrorist movement, or the explosion of information technologies. But he instinctively

---

20. *The Security/Safety Merger*, *Security World Magazine* (Cahners Publishing), Arthur E. Torrington, January, 1975 (Part I).

knew that an organization's business units needed to "move toward union or uniformity" if the job of security and safety were to be accomplished.

By November, 2005, the concept of *convergence* had culminated into a new paradigm, "Convergence of Enterprise Security Organizations." A report was commissioned by the Alliance for Enterprise Security Risk Management (AESRM), a coalition formed in February 2005 by three leading international security organizations: ASIS International (ASIS), International IT Governance Professionals (ISACA), and Information Systems Security Association (ISSA). [21] The report states in its introduction, "The Alliance was created to address the integration of traditional and information security functions and to encourage board and senior executive level attention to critical security-related issues and the need for a comprehensive approach to protect the enterprise..."

The Alliance members—who represent more than 90,000 global security professionals with broad security backgrounds and skills—recognized that such integration or convergence of security roles impacts not just the security function of a given business, but the business as a whole. Similarly, the members realized that as companies' assets become increasingly information-based and intangible, there is a greater need to integrate traditional and information security.

CONDITIONS FOR CONVERGENCE

The ASIS International definition captures this shift to the business framework by emphasizing the following language, "the identification of security risks and interdependencies between business functions and interdependencies." This change in emphasis should have a profound impact on how business unit leaders view security. Indeed, it sets the conditions to allow convergence to emerge.[22]

CONTINUING PRESSURE TO REDUCE COST

Finally, enterprises will always grapple with balancing risk/reward tradeoffs. As risk become increasingly complex, enterprise must take a systematic, pragmatic approach to security that maximizes resources while adequately managing risk. In an era of rapidly changing risks, efficient allocation of security resources requires *a risk based approach* (highlight and italics added) and greater transparency related to security

---

21. *The Alliance for Enterprise Security Risk Management,* Convergence of Enterprise Security Organizations, Booz/Allen/Hamilton, November 8, 2005.
22. *Ibid.,* Section 2.2, page 4.

strategy. What we will and will not focus on needs to be clear to avoid continual realignment based on the most "recent" set of issues, versus the most important.[23]

In another prescient article, two highly regarded corporate security directors, in 1994, wrote an article encouraging the integration of *audit* and the security functions:

Information Exchange

Improved communications between employees of both departments (audit and security) and a clear understanding of mutual roles can create a formidable force against internal and external crime. Besides structured training, regular information exchange is critical to effective coordination.

Auditors and security staff should have formal exchanges at least monthly, including preaudit discussions and a review of the results of recent investigations and audits.

Preaudit discussions between appropriate audit and security personnel ensure that audit emphasis in security-related areas is based on current exposures and losses. Auditors are routinely notified of security incidents that impact their area of responsibility. They are provided necessary details and methodology of the incident so that they may recommend alternative procedures to help prevent similar losses at other company operations.[24]

IMPERATIVES DRIVING CONVERGENCE

- Enterprises are becoming more complex in a global economy where external partners are increasing (i.e. outsourcing).
- Increasingly, value is shifting from physical to information-based assets.
- Emerging technology is creating an overlap between physical and information security functions.
- More regulations are developing in response to new threats and business interactions (e.g. Sarbanes-Oxley; Federal Sentencing Guidelines, etc.).
- Enterprises are constantly trying to efficiently mitigate risk.[25]

---

23. *Ibid.,* Section 3.1, page 8.
24. *Crossing Corporate Turf,* Gerald W. Wernz and Timothy L. Williams, 1994.
25. *The Alliance for Enterprise Security Risk Management,* Convergence of Enterprise Security Organzia-tions, Section 3.1, p. 6, Booz/Allen/Hamilton, November 8, 2005.

There are many efficiencies to be gained from enacting an integrated security operation. A few specific examples are:

1. Alignment with the organization's security business plan, mission, and philosophy.

2. More motivated security team members as a result of cross-training.

3. Higher visibility from senior leadership.

4. One-stop shopping for employees to report incidents and ask questions resulting in more comprehensive metrics and trending.

5. A more comprehensive employee security education and awareness program, identifying security risks across all discipline.[26]

In the society we live in today—with the threat of terrorism and a dramatic increase in the number and complexity of other security-related risks such as computer viruses, cyber attacks, information theft, extortion and fraud—companies must find a more comprehensive approach to protecting their employees, core networks and facilities. Through the convergence model, security professionals have a unique opportunity to elevate their role in the organization, advance the security profession, and deliver additional value to the organization through cost savings and related efficiencies.[27]

The Alliance for Enterprise Security Risk Management's (AESRM) study ("Convergence of Enterprise Security Organizations"), was put together by a coalition formed in February 2005 by three leading international security organizations: ASIS International (ASIS), International IT Governance Professionals (ISACA). This study was primarily concerned with the protection of information technology and its infrastructure. As stated in the Introduction of this book, the inclusion of an organization's culture, along with all other risk assessment modalities, is essential to an achievable and sustainable security program. *Convergence* as a total discipline implies a strong commitment to interdependence—both within an organization as well as with global organizations having similar security objectives. For the purpose of this discussion, the paradigm of *convergence* shall only be applied to the risk assessment process that uses convergence (interdependence) within a facility or a single corporate-wide organization to identify and manage potential security threats.

---

26. *New Study Finds the Convergence of Traditional and Information Security Functions Necessary for Global Organizations to Protect Assets, Maintain Profits,* ISACA, www.isaca.org, 12/13/06.
27. www.isaca.org, Timothy L. Williams, CPP, Vice President of Corporate and Systems Security for Nortel Networks member of the ASIS International Board of Directors.

HOW IS CONVERGENCE ACHIEVED?

• Use of highly motivated security focus groups (see Chapter 5, "Risk Assessment by Focus Group"). This focus group should be comprised of all strategic operating groups within a facility or organization.

• Deliver presentations to strategic operating groups. This should include high-level security training for security staff and, where applicable, invitations to other operating groups and senior management. Speakers having an excellent reputation in the convergence discipline should also be invited to speak to invigorate attendance to these sessions.

• Seek invitations to participate with other operating group planning meetings in order to learn their agenda and potential security needs. This is not a security meeting, but your opportunity to listen and learn their agenda and how security can support it.

• Construct "customer" opinion surveys. How is the security function perceived? How can it be improved? How can it become a strategic partner in providing security support to their operating agenda and personal safety/security? What are their security concerns? What security technologies are they using and how can they be more efficiently and economically merged with security's existing technology management to affect an economy?

• Develop and "market" a consultancy model that is available to all operating groups. Seek to independently identify their needs, conduct research, and offer recommendations.

• Construct a survey that requests risk data. Ask each operating group to independently list what risks have impacted their business operation or will do so in the future. Also identify those risks that each group considers relevant to their staff's security and safety. This can be linked to the "customer" opinion survey.

Process of an Integrated Risk Assessment Process

It is essential that the security function have its own mission statement and business plan. Perceptions of security are sometimes cynical or cause security managers to lack parity with other business managers. Security's role in using the *convergence* paradigm can become arduous at best if this is the case. For this reason, one of the first objectives for a security manager is to communicate its mission and objectives in a way that:

• Is perceived as a strategic management discipline.

• Identifies a value added model to the organization's mission.

- Is easily understood and relates to the philosophy and mission of the organization.
- Lays a foundation for the development and acceptance of security's agenda.
- Can be used as a training/orientation guideline.

A positive attitude must be generated by the "personality" of security's mission. This is highly relevant if they are to have a significant role in changing management's objectives. If they are business persons and participate on the management team, the answer is unequivocally **yes**. Security's function is larger than just modifying attitude through reactive strategy. Today, security managers are partners with management. They, as examples, participate in the development of business ethics programs, acquisition analysis, human resources, international relations, site selection, crisis management, facilities management, and strategic planning to name a few. It won't be much longer before this type of integration will be the norm rather than the exception. No progressive company will survive in a competitive and global marketplace if it does not integrate security management with all relevant operating groups.

INTELLIGENCE

Several years ago a multi-national manufacturing company was conducting a risk assessment using the focus group study (along with other strategies). The focus group was made up of vice presidents from each of its operating groups. The facilitator was discussing how business intelligence gathering and industrial espionage can produce a mosaic that assists in defining critical proprietary information. They were explained the simple strategy of using subterfuge phone calls to various department heads as one method of developing this mosaic. At that moment, one vice president admitted to receiving almost the identical phone call (as described by the facilitator). This was followed by a focus group chain reaction. Almost every vice president in the room joined in confirming that they also received the same call. Needless to say, an immediate investigation was conducted and it was confirmed that a competitor was attempting to illegally obtain strategic proprietary data. Had it not been for the timely focus group meeting, a significant information loss would have occurred at an enormous cost to the organization. This case speaks volumes to the necessity of security programs being formed through the use of a *convergence* paradigm. The vice presidents in the focus group, each representing different operating groups, had never integrated information security. They had never achieved "uniformity." After this security focus group meeting it was, of course, not at all difficult to convince senior management of the need to integrate information security strategies. Understanding true risk potential and its impact to each department (market share and the jobs that may have been lost) is the true catalyst to implementing an achievable and sustainable security program.

Most security risks are reasonably identifiable using standard risk assessment methodology. But others (e.g., cyber crime, anomalous and bizarre events, unique business operation threats, and the cunning of man made threats, etc.) require a far greater coordination of intelligence gathering to be identified. In this area of risk assessment, the integration of disparate operating groups within one organization or the *convergence* of industry enterprises is far more likely to identify critical threats and developing consensus for a preventive strategy.

GLOBALIZATION

Any business organization doing business globally becomes a "citizen" of the international marketplace. The business practices, political philosophy, radical religious beliefs, ethical standards, mores, and much more become a serious concern for asset protection. Integrating security management's agenda with a *convergence* paradigm throughout all overseas operations is critical for understanding the security risks.

The Overseas Security Advisory Council (OSAC) is a Federal Advisory Committee with a U.S. Government Charter to promote security cooperation between American business and private sector interests worldwide and the U.S. Department of State. OSAC currently encompasses the 34-member core Council, an Executive Office, over 100 Country Councils, and more than 3,500 constituent member organizations and 372 associates.

The objectives of the Council as outlined in the Charter are:

1. To establish continuing liaison and to provide for operational security cooperation between State Department security functions and the Private Sector.

2. To provide for regular and timely interchange of information between the Private Sector and the State Department concerning developments in the overseas security environment.

3. To recommend methods and provide material for coordinating security planning and implementation of security programs.

4. To recommend methods to protect the competitiveness of American businesses operating worldwide.

AUTHORITY

"The Council is established under authority of the Secretary of State pursuant to 22 U.S.C. 2656 and in accordance with the Federal Advisory Committee Act as amended. The activities of the Council are determined to be in the public interest and are directly related to overseas security functions of the Department of State. The increase in terrorism over the last 25 years and the continuing threat against U.S. interests overseas has forced many American companies to seek advice and assistance from the U.S. Government, particularly the State Department. In 1985, a handful of chief executive officers from prominent American companies met with then Secretary of State George P. Shultz to promote cooperation between the American private sector worldwide and the U.S. Government on security issues. The subsequent establishment of the Overseas Security Advisory Council (OSAC) has developed into an enormously successful joint venture. Today over 3,500 U.S. companies, educational institutions, religious and non-governmental organizations are constituents of OSAC. The Council provides a forum for best practices and provides the tools needed to cope with today's ever changing challenges and security related issues abroad." [28]

U.S. DEPARTMENT OF STATE

In conducting a risk assessment concerning the threats traveling abroad doesn't have to be confusing if you know the right things before you go. The U.S. Department of State Web site provides information and links to pages containing background and requirements for Americans traveling abroad. Links access an alphabetical listing of countries to view specific entry requirements. Links also include information on passports, visas, immunizations, medical information, and additional fees. The travel section also includes information concerning conditions abroad that may affect your safety and security. Other links provide additional information applicable to other security risks in the international marketplace. These links are continually updated.[29]

EXAMPLES

"Disrupting information and supplies, interrupting transportation mechanisms, or failing to meet certain compliance requirements, can lead to the dislocation of an entire product line. Consider what happed in September, 2002, when a labor dispute shut down West Coast ports for several weeks. As critical supply chains stopped

---

28. https://www.osac.gov/About/index.cfm
29. http://travel.state.gov/visa/americans/americans_1252.html

functioning normally, severely constraining manufacturing and product replenishment, U.S. companies lost an estimated $1 billion per day. One company that produces information products indicated that its decision to establish an 'external security chain of trust' came as a result of its reliance on information from other suppliers. Situations such as these demonstrate the need for developing positive relationships with external partners." [30]

The above examples illustrate the need for risk assessments being conducted in a modern and dynamic international organization. This process, in a global marketplace, must include *a convergence* paradigm.

"Increasingly, assets, whether physical or information-based, have physical and information security related risks... Converging the security management process into a *Business Security Management Process* moves the traditional physical security management or IT security management into an approach with a wider spectrum with which to plan for, monitor, and respond to vulnerabilities. This unified entity then has the capability to understand the enterprise in its entirety rather than have access to only elements pertaining to specific information or physical security concerns." [31]

CONCLUSION

"It is critical to develop relationships with people across functional boundaries to facilitate security *convergence*. Security leaders should proactively reach across functional boundaries to discover mutual projects. This action will help to reduce costs attributed to the mitigation of duplicative efforts and will increase interoperability of security functions. Senior management buy-in of business security is essential to promoting staff to follow through on implementing security measure and funding allocation. Because the ROI of business, security can be difficult to quantify, a broad understanding of the importance throughout the organization can often qualify the investment." [32]

---

30. *The Alliance for Enterprise Security Risk Management, Convergence of Enterprise Security Organizations,* Booz/Allen/Hamilton, p. 15, November 8, 2005.
31. *Ibid., p. 20.*
32. *Ibid., p. 22.*

## CHAPTER FOUR

Security Surveys
A Strategic Function of Risk Assessment

The word "survey" conjures up so many meanings and methodologies that it often is confused as being synonymous with the total function of "risk assessment." It is, of course, a strategic ingredient in performing a risk assessment. An entire text could be written on the various types and methodologies that "surveys" follow. For the purpose of this article, we are focusing and defining what a survey is and how it can best be used as part of a risk assessment's strategy. *Merriam-Webster's Collegiate Dictionary* defines "survey" as:

"To examine as to condition, situation, or value: APPRAISE." "To query (someone) in order to collect data for the analysis of some aspect of a group or area." "To view or consider comprehensively." "INSPECT, SCRUTINIZE."

"The survey is the process whereby one gathers data and reflects the who, what, how, where, when, and why of the client's existing operation. The survey is the fact-finding process."[33]

OBJECTIVES

- Perform qualitative gathering of intelligence to assist in identifying risk.
- Study target's physical attributes (subject location and surrounding community) to determine how it may contribute to the incidence of risk.
- Study target's security program, policy, and procedures and how it is supporting current strategies.
- Study security's mission and operation to determine how effective it is in deterring, detecting, delaying, denying, responding to, and/or recovering from predicable risk.
- Interview employees and other outsourced personnel to determine to what degree they are participating in the security program. Are they part of the problem or part of the solution?
- Interview senior management to get a sense of their commitment to a security program. Evaluate their lifestyles and public image to attract security risks?
- Study target's incident history to determine all (3 to 5 years) prior incidence of security events. Are these data recorded in a relational database? Can accurate analysis of these data be used for risk assessment purposes? Do these data confirm

---

33. *Security Consulting,* Charles A. Sennewald, CPP, Second Edition, Butterworth-Heinemann, 1996.

that existing corporate security strategies are mitigating risk? Do they corroborate the type of frequency of security risks.

- Study local police department criminal incident histories *and* service calls (runs) to the subject study location to evaluate the extent to which incidents are occurring, but not recorded by the target's incident history files.

- This study should also include interviews with local police and their overall impression of risk exposure to security and safety at the target. Determine if a valid police liaison program exists.

- Determine other surveys used in like and competitive organizations to identify parallel intelligence data valuable to your organization's risk assessment. Consider benchmarking as a means of identifying what risks and strategies are being used by like and competitive companies.

- Benchmarking may also be very useful in comparison to your organization's other facilities or like/competitive organizations.

- Perform research of professional and/or trade associations' media outreach. These associations sponsor studies followed by results included in academic journals, white papers, and articles. Often the subject of this outreach concerns security issues. Internet searches will also be enormously helpful in this effort.

- Perform searches with legal database resources (e.g. LexisNexis) to identify trends in civil and criminal liability exposure. These database resources provide useful history regarding your organization's exposure to litigation arising from specific security risks.

- Perform research of government studies. Familiarity with Federal Codes concerned with penalties for corporate wrongdoing may be essential in connecting the dots with other risk assessment intelligence identified. Depending upon your organization's operation, a study of the *Federal Sentencing Guidelines Manual,* Unites States Sentencing Commission, West Publishing Company, November 1, 1991, 1992 Edition, will identify the "culpability index" promulgated to quantify the civil or criminal penalty to be imposed should your organization be found guilty of offenses outlined in the guidelines.

- Listen to and study the intelligence provided by your organization's security patrol and investigation resources, not only from incident data and investigation reports, but from activity logs that identify day-to-day operational observations. If your organization does not employ security patrol, then seek a way to identify this same intelligence from your maintenance and/or janitorial operations. These data are best entered and analyzed in a relational database.

DELIVERABLES

Surveys described in this article are primarily intended for mid-size to large organizations. But a small entrepreneurial firm may be high-tech or operationally diverse and looking to become a larger organization. These firms may also need risk assessment survey skills to avoid the pitfalls of competition reducing their edge to grow.

What deliverables are derived from a survey?

• Change. Security persons on patrol are first taught to be observant in their first patrol round, but on the repeat tours must be diligent to discern differences from their original observations. Fence line damage? New car on lot? Persons loitering? New graffiti? Broken glass? They are also taught to "think outside the box." While patrolling, do they look straight ahead or in *all* directions? All risk assessment surveys discussed in this article must also seek to identify change at all levels of the organization's environment and operation.

• Risks based upon the built environment: "...Crime is not always predictable because it is the work of human scheming. In our efforts to combat the threat, it is essential that we all attempt to reduce the opportunity so often given to the criminal to commit crime. Every building, large or small, creates a potential crime risk and planners and architects owe it to their clients to devise and implement effective security measures. The subject of designing security with architects is another way of conducting a security survey, but in this case, it is before construction." [34]

"CPTED (Crime Prevention Through Environmental Design) is an attempt to reduce crime and fear in a target setting by 1) reducing criminal opportunity and 2) fostering positive social interaction among the legitimate users of that setting. The emphasis is on prevention, rather than on apprehension and punishment." [35]

• Security Awareness. Each time a survey is performed properly, key personnel are interviewed and asked to be involved in the process. Some staff are very reluctant to become involved, but when asked and briefed about the purpose of the survey they often become forthright and helpful. They are sometimes uncomfortable with the risk potential they perceive, which may include a risk to their personal safety, and are grateful for the opportunity to participate and provide their input.

---

34. *Handbook of Loss Prevention and Crime Prevention,* Lawrence J. Fennelly, Butterworth-Heinemann, Second Edition, Chapter 3, p. 37, 1989.
35. *Crime Prevention Through Environmental Design, An Operational Handbook,* National Institute of Justice, Research Report, December, 1984.

- Operational Risk. Any internal or external business operation may have foreseeable security risks. Each business has unique business operations that need to be studied both by physical survey and interviews with key personnel. The integration of operating departments (**convergence** - to be discussed in another chapter) is critical in delivering strategic risk data and responsive proactive strategies to senior management.

Risks Need to Be Discovered by Survey of Independent Resources

In February, 1998, Pinkerton's, Inc., issued a release to business editors revealing the results of their fifth annual *survey* submitted to corporate security executives. It identified what was then the 10 most important security threats. Of the top 10 most important security threats identified by security directors of Fortune 1000 companies, the first six are employee-related concerns, as seen below: (Pinkerton Survey Report).

1. Employee Theft
2. Workplace Violence
3. Fraud & White-collar Crime
4. Employee Selection
5. Hardware & Software Theft
6. Ethical Business Conduct
7. Crisis Management & Executive Protection
8. Internet Security
9. Intellectual Property Protection
10. Property Crime

In 2006, due to the 9/11 tragedy as well as the more recent concerns with "Cybercrime," the above list has probably been modified. "For its national survey, Pinkerton asked respondents to rate each of 23 listed potential security threats on a five-point scale, with five being the "most important" and one "least important." The combined responses were converted into an average for each threat and then ranked. Security questionnaires were mailed to 1,607 corporate security directors of Fortune 1000 companies in December, 1997. Of these, 137 (8.5%) were returned and are reflected in the results. It is interesting to note that this survey did reveal "...a steady rise in the perceived threat of cybercrime..." (Pinkerton Survey Report).

Surveys are normally considered to be a self evaluation of your organization's facility or corporate wide operations. However, survey resources by others will be beneficial to the risk assessment process. The example of Pinkerton's annual survey and other intelligence agencies can have an intrinsic value in evaluating potential threats to your organization, or at least objectively direct your risk assessment strategies and intelligence gathering.

SURVEY PROCESS

"...The purpose of the survey is to examine the client's physical features, procedures, activities and possible targets of criminal attack in order to recognize and appraise the specific risks which are present." [36]

" ...The purpose of the security survey is to provide the practitioner with sufficient knowledge to map out crime risk management strategies for recommendation to the client. Note the use of the word *strategies*. Although the practitioner must be concerned with detail in the survey, his overall objective is to achieve a balanced crime risk management system design. For this reason, the method of approach to the survey should also be strategic in nature." [37]

Every organization is uniquely different and will therefore have varied risk assessment survey needs. There is no one generic survey form. Any attempt to facilitate a survey using a generic form may lead to inaccurate findings. To facilitate the reader being able to evaluate the construction of a survey, the below sample is presented; but only as a *guide* to assist in developing one for your needs.

---

36. *Handbook of Loss Prevention and Crime Prevention,* Lawrence J. Fennelly, Butterworths, Second Edition, Chapter 32, p. 630, 1989
37. *Ibid.*

SAMPLE SECURITY / SAFETY FORM

Location: _____

Phone: _____ **Fax:** _____ **E-mail:** _____

Please identify any corrective action required under "Comments" column.

Inspection Objective	Ok? (Yes or No)	Comments
COMMUNITY ANALYSIS:		
Local Police Liaison:		
a. Planned contact? Meeting?	a. ☐ Yes ☐ No	
b. Does facility interact with a crime prevention officer with the local police?	b. ☐ Yes ☐ No	
c. Regularly receive local police incident history?	c. ☐ Yes ☐ No	
d. Receive alerts? Identify how.	d. ☐ Yes ☐ No	
e. Any special risks identified by local police?	e. ☐ Yes ☐ No	
f. Identify any major crimes or events in the community during the past two years that could impact this facility's security.	f. ☐ Yes ☐ No	
g. Have there been any major crimes at Facility in the past two years?	g. ☐ Yes ☐ No	

Inspection Objective	Ok? (Yes or No)	Comments
Does Facility Maintain:		
a. Hard copy incident reports. If yes, where are they stored & how are they distributed?	a. ☐ Yes ☐ No	
b. Are incident reports loaded and analyzed in a database? If yes, where and how?	b. ☐ Yes ☐ No	
Community Relationship:		
Are there any issues impacting upon the facility's relationship with the community that are problematic and may pose a security risk/problem?	☐ Yes ☐ No	
Unique Neighbor Security Issues: Are there any neighbors who present unique security risks/problems that impact the facility? If yes, identify neighbor and types of problems.	☐ Yes ☐ No	
Planned Neighboring Facilities: Are there any neighboring facilities planned that may impact the security of the facility in the future?	☐ Yes ☐ No	
Security Awareness: Does the facility have any formal security awareness program? If yes, explain the program.	☐ Yes ☐ No	

Inspection Objective	Ok? (Yes or No)	Comments
Local Media: Have any stories or related incidents involving the media affected the safety/ security of the facility? Is there a policy that clearly establishes who, how, and when the media may be spoken with at the facility?	☐ Yes ☐ No	
SECURITY OFFICER SERVICES		
Does the facility use security officer services: If yes, what type?' a. Contract Services b. Proprietary Security Force c. Hybrid Service d. Off-duty Commissioned Police Officers	☐ Yes ☐ No a. ☐ b. ☐ c. ☐ d. ☐	
How many hours per week are security officer services provided? Identify schedule to include hours covered and number of officers used for all hours covered. Attach schedule to this form.	☐ Yes ☐ No	
Does the facility's security program have a planning mechanism for **special events**?	☐ Yes ☐ No	

Inspection Objective	Ok? (Yes or No)	Comments
If contract services, obtain copy of agreement for services with any attachments. Also obtain copy of insurance certificate.	☐ Yes ☐ No	
Whether in-house or contract security, identify if the following does exist and, if necessary, explain under comments: a. Pre-service training b. In-service training c. Preemployment screening d. Supervision methodology e. Tour documentation f. Patrol vehicle? g. Two-way radio equipment If yes, speaks to whom? h. Pager? i. First Aid (Responder) Certified? j. E.M.T.? k. C.P.R.? l. Heimlich Maneuver?	☐ Yes ☐ No a. ☐ b. ☐ c. ☐ d. ☐ e. ☐ f. ☐ g. ☐ h. ☐ i. ☐ j. ☐ k. ☐ l. ☐	

Inspection Objective	Ok? (Yes or No)	Comments
Do security officers receive unannounced security inspections? a. By whom? b. How often? c. Report filed? To whom?	☐ Yes ☐ No	
Does facility use an RFP and performance standard when hiring security officer services? If yes, obtain copy of same.	☐ Yes ☐ No	
Obtain copy of the following: a. Incident Report Form b. Daily Activity Logs c. Standing Operating Proc. d. Emergency Proc. Manual e. Post Instructions f. Officers' Handbook g. Memoranda Log Book	☐ Yes ☐ No a. ☐ b. ☐ c. ☐ d. ☐ e. ☐ f. ☐ g. ☐	
OUTER FACILITY PERIMETER SECURITY:		
Is there perimeter fencing? a. Are there gaps in the fencing (identify gaps)? b. Does it conform to published standards? c. Is it in good repair?	☐ Yes ☐ No a. ☐ Yes ☐ No b. ☐ Yes ☐ No c. ☐ Yes ☐ No	

Inspection Objective	Ok? (Yes or No)		Comments
Are all shrubbery properly trimmed so that there are no convenient hiding places to the perimeter of the building or grounds?	☐ Yes	☐ No	
Can the parking lots clearly be seen from the street by passing police patrol and/or passers by?	☐ Yes	☐ No	
Are all trees properly trimmed so existing lighting is not blocked or excessively creating shadows?	☐ Yes	☐ No	
Is lighting of the facility's perimeter adequate? If not, identify where lighting needs to be improved.	☐ Yes	☐ No	
Are all lighting fixtures operative? NOTE: This will require survey of the facility during evening hours.	☐ Yes	☐ No	
Is there a set program at this facility to promptly report and replace burned out lighting fixtures (next day is considered "prompt")?	☐ Yes	☐ No	
Is there a logging process to document the lighting maintenance policy?	☐ Yes	☐ No	

Inspection Objective	Ok? (Yes or No)		Comments
Is there a logging process to document other maintenance requests that impact security and/or safety?	☐ Yes	☐ No	
Has the facility's perimeter (e.g., grounds, building facade, etc.) experienced any vandalism? If yes, describe damage under "comments."	☐ Yes	☐ No	
At time of inspection, were all common area fire exit and exit/entry doors in good repair?	☐ Yes	☐ No	
At time of inspection, were there any visible signs of tampering or other attempts to force open any of the perimeter doors or windows?	☐ Yes	☐ No	
At time of inspection were all windows locked and secured as designed?	☐ Yes	☐ No	
At time of inspection were all windows in good repair (locks, molding, and glass panes?	☐ Yes	☐ No	
Did anything about the perimeter of the facility suggest that the facility had been or would be victimized?	☐ Yes	☐ No	

Inspection Objective	Ok? (Yes or No)	Comments
PARKING AREAS		
Percentage of parking: a. Indoors? b. Outdoors?	☐ Yes ☐ No ☐ Yes ☐ No	
Are parking areas patrolled? If yes, how often? How is the patrol documented?	☐ Yes ☐ No	
Adequacy of lighting: a. Indoor Garage b. Outdoor Spaces All fair and poor lighting locations should be identified.	Indoor: ☐ Good ☐ Fair ☐ Poor Outdoor: ☐ Good ☐ Fair ☐ Poor	
If using indoor garage, is the overall security of the garage within standard security practices? If no, identify what should be improved.	☐ Yes ☐ No	
Is the overall security of the outdoor spaces within standard security practices? If no, identify what should be improved.	☐ Yes ☐ No	
Has there been any experience with vandalism of auto, theft from auto, or theft of auto? Identify history in all lots for the past two years.	☐ Yes ☐ No	

Inspection Objective	Ok? (Yes or No)		Comments
Has any of the other criminal history experienced by the facility occurred on the parking lot areas? It is particularly important to note any crimes against persons.	☐ Yes	☐ No	
Are all parking space lines well painted and defined?	☐ Yes	☐ No	
Is there any broken glass or other debris on the parking lot suggesting problems with vandals or other crime?	☐ Yes	☐ No	
Is the line of sight from one parking lane to another good or are there items (e.g. shrubs, trees, etc.) blocking the view?	☐ Yes	☐ No	
INTERIOR SECURITY AND SAFETY REQUIREMENTS:			
Do facility employees wear: a. Photo id cards? b. Worn visibly? c. Carried on person? d. Are id cards linked to an access control system?	☐ Yes ☐ Yes ☐ Yes ☐ Yes	☐ No ☐ No ☐ No ☐ No	

Inspection Objective	Ok? (Yes or No)		Comments
Does the facility have a sufficient number (and the proper type) of fire extinguishers and are they all properly charged?	☐ Yes	☐ No	
Are all fire exits properly marked?	☐ Yes	☐ No	
Does the facility have an adequate emergency evacuation plan and are the proper number of evacuation route drawings and signs prominently displayed?	☐ Yes	☐ No	
Are there fire towers in the facility?	☐ Yes	☐ No	
a. Were the towers clean and unblocked?	☐ Yes	☐ No	
b. Was each tower clearly identified with signs for evacuation?	☐ Yes	☐ No	
c. Were the fire tower doors securely closed and providing a tight integrity to smoke infiltration?	☐ Yes	☐ No	
d. Was anything being stores in the fire towers?	☐ Yes	☐ No	
Are any electrical outlets overloaded or has the facility experienced power failures or brown-outs from electrical overload of the system?	☐ Yes	☐ No	

Inspection Objective	Ok? (Yes or No)	Comments
Are any volatile substances (e.g., paint, paint thinner, kerosene, etc.) improperly stored?	☐ Yes ☐ No	
Does the building have a fire alarm system? Name of fire alarm vendor? Is the fire alarm being tested at least once each year? Is the system under a preventive maintenance contract?	☐ Yes ☐ No	
Who monitors the fire alarm system? a. Console at facility b. Remotely by alarm company c. Directly to public authority d. Audible alarm only	 ☐ Yes ☐ No ☐ Yes ☐ No ☐ Yes ☐ No ☐ Yes ☐ No	
Fire alarm consists of: a. Sprinkler (full/partial) b. Smoke Detectors c. Rate of Rise/Fixed Temp d. Pull Stations	☐ Yes ☐ No ☐ Yes ☐ No ☐ Yes ☐ No ☐ Yes ☐ No	
Have there been any persistent false alarm problems with the fire alarm system?	☐ Yes ☐ No	
Does the facility have an intrusion alarm? Where?	☐ Yes ☐ No	

Inspection Objective	Ok? (Yes or No)		Comments
Is the facility's intrusion alarm system inspected and tested at least once each year?	☐ Yes	☐ No	
Is the system under a preventive maintenance contract?	☐ Yes	☐ No	
Is the intrusion alarm remotely monitored: By whom?	☐ Yes	☐ No	
a. Console at facility	☐ Yes	☐ No	
b. Remotely by alarm company	☐ Yes	☐ No	
c. Directly to public authority	☐ Yes	☐ No	
d. Audible alarm only	☐ Yes	☐ No	
Is the fire alarm systems compatible with current ADA regulations?	☐ Yes	☐ No	
Is the intrusion alarm system compatible with current ADA regulations?	☐ Yes	☐ No	
Has the intrusion alarm system had any persistent false alarms?	☐ Yes	☐ No	
Have all key employees received proper training on the use of the intrusion alarm system?	☐ Yes	☐ No	

Inspection Objective	Ok? (Yes or No)	Comments
Does the facility have: a. Silent emergency alarms that communicate to facility security? b. Silent emergency alarms that communicate to police? c. Paging or beeper system to summon facility security?	☐ Yes ☐ No ☐ Yes ☐ No ☐ Yes ☐ No	
Does the facility have CCTV coverage in the common area? If yes, a. Monitored? b. Is it recorded?	☐ Yes ☐ No ☐ Yes ☐ No ☐ Yes ☐ No	
Are all CCTV controls for monitoring and recording secure? a. VHS recording? b. Digital Video Recording?	☐ Yes ☐ No ☐ Yes ☐ No ☐ Yes ☐ No	
Is the CCTV system under a preventive maintenance agreement?	☐ Yes ☐ No	
What is the quality of the CCTV system?	☐ Good ☐ Fair ☐ Poor	
Are CCTV cameras: a. Indoors? b. Outdoors? c. Remotely Controlled? Attach list of locations for all cctv cameras.	 ☐ Yes ☐ No ☐ Yes ☐ No ☐ Yes ☐ No	

Inspection Objective	Ok? (Yes or No)		Comments
Is CCTV system linked to any other integrated technology?	☐ Yes	☐ No	
a. Motion Detection	☐ Yes	☐ No	
b. Intelligent Motion Sensors	☐ Yes	☐ No	
c. Computer Software Control	☐ Yes	☐ No	
How does the facility control its keying and locking management program?			
a. Not At All	☐ Yes	☐ No	
b. Manually (indexed)	☐ Yes	☐ No	
d. Software	☐ Yes	☐ No	
d. In-house Maintenance	☐ Yes	☐ No	
e. Outsourced Maintenance	☐ Yes	☐ No	
f. Removable Core System?	☐ Yes	☐ No	
Does the facility use any other type of physical security system? If yes, identify type and purpose.	☐ Yes	☐ No	
Bomb Threat:			
a. Are forms available at all facility telephone that answer outside calls?	☐ Yes	☐ No	
b. Is there a formal bomb threat procedure?.	☐ Yes	☐ No	
c. Were employees of facility familiar with policy & forms?	☐ Yes	☐ No	

Inspection Objective	Ok? (Yes or No)	Comments
Are emergency telephone numbers (police, fire, ambulance, and landlord where applicable) posted?	☐ Yes ☐ No	
Are the local police and/ or alarm company central station updated of any changes to the emergency contact names and phone numbers?	☐ Yes ☐ No	
MISCELLANEOUS - SECURITY		
Do the elevators automatically return to ground level if fire alarm activates?	☐ Yes ☐ No	
Do they have intercom? To where?	☐ Yes ☐ No	
Are cleaning services for common areas of facility: a. Contracted? b. In-House?	a. ☐ b. ☐	
Are cleaning services for parking lots: a. Contracted? b. In-House? If services are contracted, identify how reports of potential security problems (evidence of victimization) are reported to facility.	a. ☐ b. ☐	

Inspection Objective	Ok? (Yes or No)	Comments
Are maintenance services: a. Contracted? b. In-House? If maintenance services are contracted, identify how reports of potential security problems (evidence of victimization) are reported to facility.	a. ☐ b. ☐	
Are all outsourced or contracted services personnel required to be screened. If yes, how?	☐ Yes ☐ No	
Are employees required to receive a preemployment screening? If yes, how?	☐ Yes ☐ No	
Is there access to the facility's roof? a. From inside facility? b. From outside facility? c. Are ladders easily available that could be used for access to the roof?	 ☐ Yes ☐ No ☐ Yes ☐ No ☐ Yes ☐ No	

NOTE: This above sample (table format) was chosen as it allows the flexibility to insert or delete inspection objectives, thereby allowing you to tailor the survey to your organization's facility or corporate wide operations.

SUGGESTIONS FOR CONDUCTING A SURVEY

- Never rely on the results of a survey from a different facility. Most environments are dynamic. It is the *change* in your environment that will provide useful intelligence to your risks assessment process.
- Surveys must be repeated on a studied frequency.
- The first survey may need internal or external consultation to initiate and facilitate the start of the process. But it is strategic that this process be eventually turned over to security operations or maintenance/janitorial personnel. They are often closest to the facility and its operation and often have the advantage in "seeing" the problem. They must be guided by a detailed survey form similar to the sample above.
- Frequency of surveys is a function of understanding your business operation and security needs. Risks in certain organizations are dynamic and surveys may need to be performed frequently. Others will not require this frequency, but no risk assessment survey should be delayed beyond one year. As most items in the survey process are repetitive and lack specificity to strategic risk changes, your survey for repeat use may be modified for monthly or quarterly usage and only the full survey used once each year. Again, it depends upon your organization and the risk intelligence identified in other risk assessment strategies.
- There is a tendency to "file" survey data. This is similar to filing loss reports. Data *must be shared and analyzed.* There is no purpose in conducting surveys and risk assessments unless the data is discussed with a security group or other management who may "see" the intelligence in a very different light. Risk intelligence that is filed away may some day prove to be a "smoking gun," but data studied and reviewed with responsive comments, memoranda, and strategies mitigates culpability and vastly improves your security program.

## CHAPTER FIVE

Risk Assessment by Focus Group

There are many paradigms to be used in conducting risk assessments, but one of the most productive strategies, in the holistic process of risk assessment, is the involvement of an organization's *security focus group* (Delphi Technique).

RATIONALE

When risk assessments are conducted solely by internal or external consultants using well recognized strategies, a vacuum may occur. The exclusion of an organization's employees, senior management, and outsourced services isolates the pivotal ownership that must occur in the development of new or upgraded security programs. Those who contribute to an idea take ownership. Those who view the ideas of others must first overcome their instinctive reticence to the rationale for ideas they didn't participate with. They are also involved in a busy agenda and are naturally reluctant to add a new objective. Therefore the inclusion of an organization's culture, along with all other risk assessment modalities, is essential to an achievable and sustainable security program.

"No security plan or program can be effective unless based upon a clear understanding of the actual risks it faces. This statement should be the basis for all security activity. Until the actual threat to assets is assessed accurately, precautions and countermeasures—even those of the highest quality, reliability, and repute—cannot be chosen, except by guess work. The value of a security program depends as much upon the relevance of resources as upon their high quality. *First* understand the problem; *then* consider solutions." [38]

"Most security decisions are complicated, involving multiple players with their own subjective assessments of security. Moreover, each of these players also their own agenda, often having nothing to do with security, and some amount of power in relation to the other players. In analyzing any security solution, we need to assess these agendas and power relationships. The question isn't which system provided the optimal security trade-offs–rather, it's which system provided the optimal security trade-offs for which players." [39]

"Personnel who are not directly involved in the analysis process must be prepared to provide information and assistance to those who are conducting it and, in addition, to abide by any procedures and limitations of activity that may result from survey activity. Management should leave no doubt that it intends to rely on the final product and base its security decision on the findings of the risk-analysis team. The

38. *Protection of Assets Manual,* Mike Knoke, editor, ASIS International, Alexandria, VA, 2004.
39. *Beyond Fear, Thinking Sensibly About Security in an Uncertain World,* Bruce Schneier, Copernicus Books, Chapter 3, p. 33., 2003.

scope of the project should be defined, and the statement of scope should specifically spell out the parameters and depth of the analysis..." [40]

"Senior management must validate a team assessment program because it requires a substantial time commitment by managers and other personnel and because it can appear to invade the "territorial imperative" of these managers. Utilizing the team approach is impossible without the full support of senior management." [41]

FACILITATION

Security focus groups are facilitated by internal or external consultants who must have sufficient knowledge and experience with security management issues. Facilitators do not lead the focus group, but are trained to *facilitate* so they may encourage group member participation. This will be a catalyst to their awareness of all security issues (e.g., definitions, strategies, risks, etc.). For example, "burglary" or "robbery" have different meanings to a lay person. It is important to level the playing field so that all focus group members understand the values they are studying and opining. Facilitators educate and encourage input from each member as they are mindful of each member's experience and knowledge. When the facilitator sits down with the security focus group, they must have an intrinsic understanding of the facility's physical layout and operational flow. The facilitator should also have, from years of experience, some understanding as to what the strategic risks are likely to be. Facilitation of the security focus group should **not** occur until the facilitator has first conducted a survey and study of the incident history, and interviews with key personnel, are completed. External consultants have the advantage of not being known by the organization being studied. They are independent and therefore carry no baggage. However, internal consultants already have an intrinsic knowledge base of their facilities, both procedurally and physically. Which type of facilitator to use will depend upon the internal consultant's ability to maintain an independent status while providing facilitation as well as being experienced and at ease with the facilitation process. If it is considered more productive to use an outsourced facilitator, then time should be allowed for that facilitator to survey and become familiar with existing physical security facilities/systems and security policy and procedures.

"In all but the smallest organization, it is impossible to expect one person to be familiar with every detail of the operation, the characteristics of its assets and its security and related exposures. Consequently, it is important to base the vulnerability

---

40. *Effective Security Management,* Charles A. Sennewald, Butterworth-Heinemann, Fourth Edition, Chapter 17, pp. 196, 2004.
41. *Protection of Assets Manual,* Mike Knoke, Editor, ASIS International, Chapter 2, Part I, p. 29.

assessment on the full range of knowledge and experience that is available within the organization."[42]

OBJECTIVES OF A SECURITY FOCUS GROUP

1. Develop intelligence for foreseeable security risks from sources closest to the organization's operational base.

2. Develop the organization's internal resources necessary to become part of the security program's solution.

3. Develop *ownership* in security program development by employees and outsourced services.

4. Develop a resource (security focus group) that is available to senior management and/or corporate security departments in future analytical needs.

SECURITY FOCUS GROUP COMPOSITION

Every organization is uniquely different, and the composition of a security focus group must be constructed carefully. The following constructs should be weighed in this process:

- Representation from all operating groups. If the target for study is one facility, then only that facility's operational participation should be considered. It is often difficult to mix multi-facility representation as each has its own unique vulnerabilities (e.g., location, demographics, business operations, etc.). However, if the risk assessment will be a *company-wide* study, then an entirely different construct must be established; governed by the corporate mission, philosophy, and security needs.

- Representatives participating with a security focus group should have tenure with their organization or facility. It is their experience and knowledge that will be strategic to the study process.

- Representatives should also be mid-level managers. It is difficult to appoint entry-level positions and at the same time obtain constructive feedback about operations. Senior managers, unless the entire focus group is made up of same, tend to mute the feedback of middle management.

---

42. *Ibid.*, Chapter 2, Part II, p.28.

- Representative should be perceived as *leaders* within their business operation. Security focus groups, depending upon the facility or organization studied, are asked to involve their department's staff in responding to the focus group surveys. The security focus group member must have the ability to carry the message to their peers.

SECURITY TASK FORCE STUDY PROCESS

There are four distinct studies that must be conducted in this process:

1. **Vulnerability Analysis.** In this stage all focus group members are introduced to a list of potential risks that may occur at their facility or organization. This list usually involves approximately sixty (60) risks. Each will be studied and graded independently by focus group members and their department staff. This article will later identify the more likely list of risks, but it is important to note that the compilation of this list requires close coordination with those who are sponsoring the study. Every organization's potential risks are uniquely different. This task should be done carefully to avoid political concerns.

2. **Opportunity Analysis:** Once it is understood what risks will be studied, it is then necessary to view each risk from the perspective of how "easy" or "difficult" it will be to occur when considering the existing security plan, policy, procedures, and political resistance. Focus group members may not entirely realize the inference of this stage of the survey, but if done carefully it will provide excellent feedback as to their opinions and comments concerning existing security strategies.

3. **Impact Analysis:** This analysis asks each focus group member to evaluate and measure the impact to persons in the facility or to the organization or facility. They are offered examples that compare risks such as graffiti (high probability in some environments, but with low impact to persons or organizations) with a major fire (low probability in most facilities, but with a significant potential impact to persons or the organization).

4. **Defensive Strategy Survey:** Once all of the risks are queued by likelihood, opportunity, and impact (see page 92), a second survey is studied by the focus group (see page 103). By this stage, security focus group members are aware and knowledgeable of potential risks and their impact to their organization, to themselves, and to their departments. In this second survey, all potential defensive strategies that may be used to deter, detect, delay, deny, respond to, and/or recover from each risk is introduced to focus group members ("security management toolbox"). These strategies are carefully explained to the focus

group so they understand their operational capability and cost. Members are asked to look at each risk and choose defensive strategies in the priority of their relevance to each risk. It is not necessary that all strategies be used; only those that have the potential for deterring, detecting, delaying, denying, responding to, and/or recovering from the risk occurrence. This second survey is usually where focus group members voice their concerns for political or operational interference with their agenda and compromises are developed to design the most effective strategies.

"Risk Management Process Flow

Step 1. Asset Assessment. Step 1 is where you identify the various assets and the loss impacts:

1.1: Determine critical assets requiring protection.

1.2: Identify undesirable events and expected impacts.

1.3: Value/prioritize assets based on the consequence of loss.

Step 2. Threat Assessment. Here we identify and characterize the threats:

2.1: Identify the threat categories and adversaries:

2.2: Assess the intent and motivation of known or suspicious adversaries.

2.3: Assess the capabilities of an adversary or threat.

2.4: Determine the frequency of threat-related incidents based on the historical data.

2.5: Estimate the degree of threat relative to each critical asset.

Step 3. Vulnerability Assessment. The identification and characterization of vulnerabilities:

3.1: Identify potential vulnerabilities related to specific assets or undesirable events.

3.2: Identify existing countermeasures in place and their level of effectiveness in reducing vulnerabilities.

3.3: Estimate the degree of vulnerability relative to each asset and threat.

Step 4. Risk Assessment. To assess risk and determine your priorities for asset protection:

4.1: Estimate the degree of impact relative to each critical asset.

4.2: Estimate the likelihood of attack by a potential adversary/threat.

4.3: Estimate the likelihood that a specific vulnerability will be exploited.

4.4: Aggregate the degree of impact (asset value) with the likelihood of a successful attack (threat x vulnerability) to determine your relative degree of risk.

Step 5. Countermeasures Assessment. Identify countermeasures, costs, and trade-offs, and select an appropriate protection strategy:

5.1: Identify potential countermeasure to reduce vulnerabilities.

5.2: Identify each countermeasure capability and effectiveness.

5.3: Identify countermeasure costs.

5.4: Conduct a countermeasure cost-benefit and trade-off analysis.

5.5: Prioritize your options and prepare appropriate recommendations for senior level management decision-maker."[43]

SECURITY FOCUS GROUP SURVEYS

Vulnerability Analysis Survey Instructions

Security management risks/issues are incidents or circumstances that cause injury or loss to the assets of your organization or facility. Your facility or organization's assets are:

1) PEOPLE; 2) INFORMATION; 3) PROPERTY; 4) REPUTATION.

The enclosed survey lists security issues and specific risks that have occurred at similar facilities throughout the country during the past two years. Listing of each risk does **not** imply that they have occurred at your organization or that it is suggested they will. Any risk or issue the focus group considers to be irrelevant to your organization or facility should be deleted. If you feel a security issue or risk has been omitted, please use the last page of this survey to add these. Score them in the same manner. At the conclusion of the survey is a space for remarks.

---

43. *Risk Management for Security Professionals,* Carl A. Roper, Butterworth-Heinemann, Chapter 3, pp. 20-21, 1999.

Column #1, Likelihood Rating

What is the likelihood that the listed risk or issue will occur? It is recognized that all listed risks are possible, but in measuring their "likelihood", ask yourself, "What do you consider to be a reasonable expectation that the risk or issue will occur or be a problem for your organization or facility compared to all the other risks listed?" Read *all* risks carefully before making any comparisons. The more likely you feel the risk or issue will occur, the higher you should rank that risk/issue in comparison to others (1 = least likely to 5 = most likely).

Column #2, Opportunity For Risk to Occur

In addition to determining your opinion as to the likelihood of a risk occurring, this survey is also attempting to learn what the *opportunity* is for the risk/issue to occur. This measurement asks you to examine your organization or facility's physical security and security policy and procedures to opine as to whether you consider them sufficiently adequate to mitigate the opportunity for the listed risk/issue to occur. Once again, compare the opportunity for this risk to occur with all others listed. If you consider the strategies in place *insufficient* to deter, detect, delay, deny, respond to and/or recover from their occurrence, you should be scoring the opportunity higher than a risk you feel is being adequately managed. In essence, you are comparing and scoring the *current* capability of your organization or facility to deter, detect, delay, deny, respond to, and/or recover from the risk. The more *opportunity* there is for the risk to occur, the higher you should rank that risk/issue in comparison to others (1 = least likely to 5 = most likely).

Column #3, Impact From Risk to Your Organization or Facility

If the risk does occur, what will be the impact to your organization? In measuring "impact" to your organization, consider that each risk or incident we are asking you to study could create a serious injury or loss to your organization or facility's information, property or reputation. Compare this impact to all other risks or issues and then score your answer. The more impact you believe will occur from each risk in the operation of your organization or facility, the higher you should rank that risk/issue in comparison to others (1 = least impact to 5 = serious impact).

Column #4, Impact to You or Other Persons

If the risk you are rating does occur, what will be the impact to you, employees, contractors, and visitors? Think in terms of how the incident would affect you and other persons (e.g., personal injury, staff morale, peace of mind, etc.). The more impact you believe will occur from each risk to you or other persons, the higher you should rank that risk/issue in comparison to others (1 = least impact to 5 = serious impact).

Notes

1. Several security issues as well as security incident types are listed (e.g. Disaster Recovery). What we are asking you to evaluate with these issues that are listed is, "What if we did have a specific crisis and your organization did not have any (or an inadequate) disaster recovery or crisis management plan in effect? What would the impact be to your organization (Column #3) or to you and others (Column #4)? This answer will bear to your opinion as to whether existing crisis management programs are adequate (or non-existent). The likelihood and opportunity scoring for these issues will be dependent upon the existence of special plans and your opinion as to their ability to reduce injury or asset loss once the incident occurs.

2. When scoring, please do not use fractions lower than a half fraction. The following may be used: 1.00/1.50/2.00/2.50/3.00/3.50/4.00/4.50/5.00.

Note

The above instructions are a *sample* of what instructions the security focus group would receive at the beginning of the first meeting. The above may be different, depending upon your organization's operation and security needs.

VULNERABILITY ANALYSIS SURVEY SAMPLE

Please do not respond in shaded areas.

Risk or Security Issue	Column #1, Likelihood to Occur 1 = Least, 5 = Most	Column #2, What Opportunity Exists For This Risk to Occur? 1 = Least, 5 = Most
1. ABUSE (PHYSICAL OR VERBAL)		
By insider		
By outsider		
2. ALCOHOLISM		
By outsider		
By insider		
3. COMPUTER SECURITY RISKS (EXCLUDING EQUIPMENT THEFT)		
Hacking/Cracking		
Unauthorized Usage		
Viruses		
Vandalism (sabotage)		
Cybercrime		
Identity Theft		
4. CRIMES AGAINST PERSONS AND PROPERTY		
Arson to facilities		
Aggravated Assault inside facilities		
Aggravated Assault outside facilities		

Column #3, Impact to Organization 1 = Least, 5 = Most	Column #4, Impact to Persons 1 = Least, 5 = Most

Please do not respond in shaded areas.

Risk or Security Issue	Column #1, Likelihood to Occur 1 = Least, 5 = Most	Column #2, What Opportunity Exists For This Risk to Occur? 1 = Least, 5 = Most
Burglary of facilities)		
Robbery - inside facilities		
Robbery - outside facilities		
Sexual Assault - inside facilities		
Sexual Assault - outside facilities		
Theft - personal property inside facilities		
Theft - personal property outside facilities		
Theft - organization property inside facilities		
Theft - organization property outside facilities		
Trespassing by person(s) into facilities (unauthorized)		
5. CROWD CONTROL ISSUES		
Demonstrations - general		
Demonstrations - organization related		
6. DANGEROUS SUBSTANCE ABUSE		
By outsider		
By insider		

Column #3, Impact to Organization 1 = Least, 5 = Most	Column #4, Impact to Persons 1 = Least, 5 = Most

Please do not respond in shaded areas.

Risk or Security Issue	Column #1, Likelihood to Occur 1 = Least, 5 = Most	Column #2, What Opportunity Exists For This Risk to Occur? 1 = Least, 5 = Most
7. DISASTER RECOVERY (failure to have adequate disaster recovery or crisis management programs) for:		
Computer system failure (software or hardware)		
Loss of telecommunications for voice or data		
Major Fire		
Other major casualty to facilities (to include natural disasters)		
Responding to violent or potentially violent criminal acts at facilities		
8. HUMAN/CIVIL RIGHTS VIOLATIONS		
To outsider		
To insider		
9. SABOTAGE to Equipment (other than computer equipment)		
By outsider		
By insider		

Column #3, Impact to Organization 1 = Least, 5 = Most	Column #4, Impact to Persons 1 = Least, 5 = Most

Please do not respond in shaded areas.

Risk or Security Issue	Column #1, Likelihood to Occur 1 = Least, 5 = Most	Column #2, What Opportunity Exists For This Risk to Occur? 1 = Least, 5 = Most
10. SEXUAL HARASSMENT		
By outsider		
By insider		
11. THREATS (TERRORISTIC)		
Bomb threat		
Threats inside facilities		
Threats outside		
12. THEFT OF PROPRIETARY INFORMATION BY ANY MEANS		
13. TRANSPORTATION SECURITY ISSUES		
Hijacking of Company Trucks		
Hijacking of Common Carrier		
Theft from trailers docked at shipping/ receiving		
Theft of trucks/ equipment		

Column #3, Impact to Organization 1 = Least, 5 = Most	Column #4, Impact to Persons 1 = Least, 5 = Most

Please do not respond in shaded areas.

Risk or Security Issue	Column #1, Likelihood to Occur 1 = Least, 5 = Most	Column #2, What Opportunity Exists For This Risk to Occur 1 = Least, 5 = Most
14. WEAPONS* OFFENSES		
Carrying concealed on person		
Concealing weapon in personal vehicle		
Concealing weapon inside facilities		
Threatening other person with weapon		
Displaying weapon (not in threatening manner to others		
15. OTHER _____		
16. OTHER _____		

* "Weapon" specifically refers to a handgun, rifle, or shotgun. Knives that are obviously offensive (hunting knife size) as well as other potentially offensive devices (e.g., police baton, billy club, etc.) should also be considered a "weapon."

Scoring The Vulnerability Survey:

The usual method of scoring is performed in a database, but can be scored manually. Each column is weighted separately. Most usually, likelihood is given a neutral weighting (1.0), opportunity is given a 1.5x weighting, impact to the organization or facility is given a 2.0x weighting; impact to persons is given a 2.5 times score. Depending upon your organization or facility, this weighting may be

Column #3, Impact to Organization 1 = Least, 5 = Most	Column #4, Impact to Persons 1 = Least, 5 = Most

different. Using the risk "**Carrying a Concealed Weapon**" as an example, the focus group scoring may have been:

Risk:	Focus GroupSurvey Score	Final Weighted Score
Likelihood	2	2.00
Opportunity	5	7.50
Impact to organization	5	10.00
Impact to persons	5	12.50
Score		**30.00**

Surveys of this nature can also evaluate independent values, such as "opportunity." Organizations often want to know the perception of the security focus group concerning their *attitude* to existing security strategies.

DEFENSIVE STRATEGY SURVEY INSTRUCTIONS

The below **"Defensive Strategy Survey"** takes each of the previously surveyed and queued risks (in order of their priority scoring) and asks you to match up the most appropriate defensive strategies to **deter, detect, delay, deny, respond to, and/or recover from** their occurrence.

Below with these instructions are a list and explanation of various defensive strategies. Their listing does not infer that LMC or your organization recommends or supports these strategies. Please read all strategies carefully before starting the survey.

In the **"Defensive Strategy Ranking"** columns (#1 through #7), please indicate **ALL** defensive strategies you consider would be economically and operationally appropriate (achievable and sustainable) at your facility to *DETER, DETECT, DENY, RESPOND TO OR RECOVER FROM* the risk or situation. **When you place each defensive strategy in these columns (#1 through #7), please do so in the order of their importance. Place the most important first (#1) to the least important (#7).** You do not have to use all defensive strategies for each listed security risk or situation. Use only those you and those assisting you consider to be economically and operationally effective in preventing the risk from occurring. If you consider that the strategy is not *ACHIEVABLE or SUSTAINABLE, do not* insert their number into the column for that risk.

The choice of defensive strategies "10," "11" or "12," for a listed risk or situation is the *only* choice that should be made when you and those assisting you consider that a risk or situation requires a *"special"* study by your organization. When you choose 10, 11 or 12, you and those assisting you would be saying that a special study of that risk or situation should be conducted and reviewed by senior management before any defensive strategies are implemented.

Defensive Strategy Survey

Rank	Security Risk/Situation	Total Score	1	2	3	4	5	6	7
#	Results of Vulnerability Assessment are listed in this column in the order of their priority.								
1	Abuse (physical or verbal)								

The above survey would list *all* risks queued by the focus group in the order of their priority. This sample provides only one sampled risk that was scored as an example.

LIST OF DEFENSIVE STRATEGIES		
#	DEFENSIVE STRATEGY	DESCRIPTION OF DEFENSIVE STRATEGY
1.	Unarmed/Uniformed (or not uniformed) <u>Contract</u> Security Officers	Use of CONTRACT security officers conducting patrol of the premises. Contract security officers serve as a deterrent and as an early alert. They are not police officers. They have no arrest authority or special police training. Supervision and training of the security officer will be provided by the contract security agency. Oversight of all such services will be provided by the contract private security agency. Quality control is maintained.
2.	Unarmed/uniformed (or not uniformed) Proprietary (in-house) Security Officers	Use of PROPRIETARY security officers conducting patrol of the premises. Proprietary security officers serve as a deterrent and as an early alert. They are not police officers. They have no arrest authority or special police training. Supervision and training of the security officer will be provided by your organization. They are employed by your organization.

LIST OF DEFENSIVE STRATEGIES		
#	DEFENSIVE STRATEGY	DESCRIPTION OF DEFENSIVE STRATEGY
3.	**Preemployment Screening of PSECU Applicants and Temporary Services**	Does your organization conduct adequate preemployment screening? There are various types of preemployment screening services (e.g., background investigations, skills testing, physical examinations, dangerous substance abuse screening, psychological testing, etc.). This strategy implies that a study and then implementation (or upgrade) to your organization's existing preemployment screening policy is necessary, but within the ethical and philosophical constraints of your organization. It must also be in conformance with all state, local, and federal legislation.
4.	**Security Awareness Programs for Employees, Temps, and other Contractors**	This defensive strategy implies that employees of your organization, temps, and contractors must be part of the solution by being aware of security issues so they make take appropriate avoidance action and/or respond to or report any suspicious activity. Senior management initiates security policy and procedures that help to implement: • Understanding security issues and potential risks • Recognizing and Reporting suspicious circumstances • Reporting all and recording all security incidents in a database • Disseminating security alerts to employees • Avoiding security risks

LIST OF DEFENSIVE STRATEGIES		
#	DEFENSIVE STRATEGY	DESCRIPTION OF DEFENSIVE STRATEGY
5.	Security Hardware	Security hardware (e.g., closed circuit television; access control; intrusion alarms, safes, locks, etc.). You do not need to know which hardware is appropriate, but if you believe that "target hardening" (use of physical controls to limit opportunity to loss) will prevent the risk then choose this strategy.
6.	Control and Monitoring of a Potential Security Risk by senior management.	Choosing this strategy implies that you consider the risk or issue may also be prevented by senior management's participation. If you do choose this strategy, you are indicating that the risk or situation should involve stewardship by senior management preparing new or enforcing existing security policy and procedures. You are asking management to add their stewardship to the policy and procedures, enforce its implementation, and to include adherence to security polices and procedures as part of each employees' performance evaluation.
7.	Employee Photo I.D. badges worn BY EMPLOYEES DISPLAYED ON THEIR PERSON AT ALL TIMES WHILE ON the organization's property.	New employee I.D. badge system to coordinate with other security technology. Badges must be visibly worn by employees at all times employees are present on the facility. This strategy implies that policy and procedures for an employee I.D. badging system will be implemented and enforced by senior management.
8.	Employee Photo I.D. badges carried by employees and presented upon request or by new policy/ procedures.	New employee I.D. badge system to coordinated with other security technology. Badges are to be carried by employees at all times. Employee will present their badge while on the facility upon request or in accordance with new policy and procedures.

	LIST OF DEFENSIVE STRATEGIES	
#	DEFENSIVE STRATEGY	DESCRIPTION OF DEFENSIVE STRATEGY
9.	Visitor and Contractor I.D. and Access Control Policy and Procedures	All visitors and contractors (temporary or regular) will be required to wear appropriate I.D. on their person at all times while they are on the organization's property. This strategy implies that strict policy and procedures for visitors and contractors will be implemented and enforced by senior management.
10.	Safeguarding Proprietary Information Study and Program Development	Selection of this strategy implies that the existing protection program for the listed information risk is not adequate in preventing the loss of proprietary data. Senior management should initiate a study of the risk and set in motion a company-wide program for the safeguarding of this proprietary information.
11.	Special Crisis Management/ Disaster Recovery Program Studied and Implemented	If you choose this strategy, you are indicating that the *existing* crisis management program for the listed crisis is *not adequate* and that a study and implementation of a new initiative is required.
12.	Special Security Programs (other than safeguarding proprietary information or crisis management programs).	If you choose this strategy, you are suggesting that the listed risk is significant to your organization and that strategies listed above would not be adequate in deterring, detecting, denying and or responding to Proprietary Information risks. You are therefore recommending that a special study be sponsored by senior management before any other defensive strategy is implemented or updated.

LIST OF DEFENSIVE STRATEGIES		
#	DEFENSIVE STRATEGY	DESCRIPTION OF DEFENSIVE STRATEGY
13.	Insert any other strategy that does not apply to the above that you believe would be productive in supporting a security program at your organization.	Describe how your strategy would work.

Once each of the defensive strategies has been entered into the above survey by the focus group, they are scored as to their frequency of selection and weighted accordingly. Defensive Strategies #10, #11, and #12 (see above) are scored separately as they do not statistically compare with all other strategies.

SUMMARY AND CONCLUSIONS

- As mentioned in the Introduction, there are many productive strategies to use in conducting risk assessments. The use of a security focus group is only one suggested format to ensure that the grass root intelligence of an organization is included. The process will educate the security focus group and foster, through the survey process, an excellent security awareness of organizational resources. It will also provide an excellent resource to future security analysis.

- The security focus group process will normally take about 40 hours—spread over a two to three month cycle. It is imperative to conveniently work this process into the schedule and agenda of the focus group and their departmental staff.

- The choice of whether the internal or external facilitator should also be used when focus group members return to their department to continue the survey process is a subjective choice and will depend upon the nature of the organization and budgetary considerations. As long as the internal facilitator is appropriately briefed, this should be no problem.

- If senior management is not interested in a facility-wide or corporate wide process, this process can also be used to study individual departments of an organization (e.g. I.T., Shipping and Receiving, etc.).

Over the past 15 years, over 25 organizations have used the security focus group process as part of their risk assessment strategy with excellent results. The objective is secure, usable intelligence to adequately assess risk and foster security awareness. To these ends the process has been popular and successful.

## CHAPTER SIX

Incident Reporting and Data Management

Most security practitioners will agree that the more data you have and the more capable you are in analyzing these data, the more effectively and accurately a risk assessment will be in planning an achievable and sustainable security program.

WHAT IS INCIDENT OR LOSS REPORTING?

Response based agencies (e.g., public emergency services or private security management, etc.), require some form of data collection process to document the record of events. These processes and programs can range from very advanced and comprehensive incident management systems purchased from commercial vendors, in-house developed database programs, or something as simple as a manual paper and pen based incident or occurrence report process.

DOCUMENTING THE RECORD OF EVENTS

No matter which format or program is chosen, the end result of incident reporting is to meet the primary goal of documenting the What, Where, When, Who, Why, and How of each incident, and most importantly, **how much**. Known as documenting the record of events, the collection of these data will have further down stream advantages in analyzing prior history to the benefit of strategic risk assessment.

In many organizations, the historical record represents the primary use of incident reporting. As incidents occur and organizations record the details, the record is referred to and read by other organization staff or management. It may be the same day or shortly thereafter to get an understanding of the particular incident. Or, it may be years down the road when the organization becomes involved in a legal proceeding (after-the-fact analysis) based on an event that has occurred within the organization. The historical records also provide details of actions taken (or not taken) by certain individuals during the incident.

What is often overlooked with Loss/Incident Reporting is the difficulty in getting an organization's staff to consistently provide a report of **all** incidents occurring. In some high-risk environments, "suspicious activity" is also sought (after careful training and orientation). Employees and outsourced personnel are naturally reluctant to provide this information. As examples:

- It may identify poor management technique that the employee doesn't want to divulge (job performance rating);
- The employee being asked to report a loss or incident may not wish to cause trouble for the person(s) who are involved.

As these and other excuses represent very few persons in an organization, it is essential to provide a strong rationale for the loss reporting system that includes a statement from senior management supporting same. It may not be achievable or sustainable to obtain 100 percent participation, but if it is added to h.r. policy and procedures, the losses being experienced in an organization will be identified (+/- a small percentage).

What Should Be Documented?

In all incident management programs, incident reporting methods will always have common features. Senior management, in their security procedures, must insist that *all* security incidents and observations (having the potential to cause losses) be included in the reporting process.

To define in more detail what is collected in an incident report, we can break each section of the incident report down into particular details:

When: There are a few key metrics in this section of the report:
  Date and Time:
  Records the date, day, and time the incident occurred.
  • Occurred 'To' [Date] and Time: Represents a 'span of time' from one time period starting on one date and ending on another.
  • Reported Date and Time: Represents the date and the time the incident was reported (for example, the date and time someone called security to report a theft).
  • Report Entered Date and Time: The date and time that the incident was entered into the system.
  • Report Closed Date and Time: Represents the date and time the incident or investigation was Closed

What: This section is generally used to describe various attributes of the incident:
  Nature of the Event:
  • Describes the type of incident (e.g., Theft, Fraud, Accident, etc.). This can be generic or may be very detailed depending on how advanced the incident reporting system being used is.
  • Incident Synopsis or Summary:
  • Describes in text a summary of the incident.
  • Incident Items:

One of the keys of 'what' was involved in an incident may also represent what was lost, stolen, or damaged (both tangible and intangible items). This list of what was lost, stolen, or damaged will be combined and related to loss information (later described)

- Reference Number: Is a unique identifying number for the particular incident.

Where: This section of incident reporting is used to describe various facets of the incident location, but an important note is that 'where' may go beyond the physical location.

- Physical Location: It is strategic to identify where *within* the subject location the incident occurred. If the incident occurred on the perimeter of the property, it is equally as essential to identify as carefully as possible where it occurred. For example, entering the building and not *where* in the building the incident occurred is only half the intelligence needed.

Who: Generally known as the 'involvements' section of an incident report, this will track two key areas:

Involved Persons:

This section will track all persons involved in the incident and various details in respect to the involved person, including but not limited to:

- Person Details: Generally Last Name, First Name and any available personal details (Date of Birth, Identification Numbers, Contact Information, Unique features and descriptors).

  Note: Several privacy laws may dictate what information can or can't be collected about an involved person and the use of such information in respect to the dissemination or sharing of the information.

- Person Involvement Type: Identifies the involvement in each incident. Recognizing that the same person may be involved in one or more incidents, each instance is tracked under generally accepted guidelines as:
  - Complainant
  - Victim
  - Witness
  - Suspect
  - Subject of Interest

Involved Organizations:

This section will track all organizations involved in the incident and their appropriate details and involvements similar to what is listed above.

An involved organization may be described as:

• Responding Agencies: Such as police, fire, EMS, tow companies that actively respond to the incident to provide a service.

• Generic Involvement: In the case of many incidents, the organization itself may be represented as any of the five involvement types listed above.

• External Organizations or Groups: This may represent a series of different types of organization that may or may not be official such as Organized Crime Groups or Activist Groups (in which involved persons listed above are involved or associated to).

Involved Vehicles:

Although some may consider this under a 'what', a vehicle is generally described as a 'who' given that a vehicle has many unique identities beyond such things as Year, Make, Model, and Style including License plates and VINs (Vehicle Identification Markers). This is inclusive of motor vehicles, boats and ships, aircraft and other vehicles (commercial heavy equipment, ATV etc).

Why: In general terms, the why is one of the most overlooked yet most important factors of incident reporting? Known under many other terms such as Outcome, Cause or Root Cause, Result, …all pieces of this puzzle allow us to put a determining factor or factors toward the incident and the corrective actions assigned to correct the cause.

• In many 'major incident' reports such as airline crashes, coroner inquests, or other major events, the Why becomes the most important attribute to relay to those who have interest in the event as it allows or supports liability or negligence claims.

• In other sectors, the Why, or the result of Why, represents the actions we take going forward and the measurements put in place to ensure the Why does not happen again or that mitigating factors are put in place if the incident does occur again.

• In many scenarios, there may be multiple contributing factors (primary and secondary causes) that contribute to an event.

• Some basic descriptors for Why tracking can be listed as (but not limited to) such things as:

  • Deliberate or Intentional
  • Unintentional Act
  • Intentional Failure to Act
  • Unintentional Failure to Act

And/Or:
- Mechanical Failure
- Policy Violation
- Careless Actions
- Tampering
- Unsafe Condition
- Undetermined
- Any list or combination of the lists above may be organizational, industry, or legislation specific.

How: In respect to Why, How is generally interrelated based upon the type of incident. Why represents the root cause of the event, How represents the formal actions of the event.

- For example: In some incidents it may be the Method of Operation and in others it may be a description of an actual mechanical failure, and still in others a description of the chain of events over a combination of factors that represent the story of 'how' the events unfolded or occurred.
- Combined with Why, these two factors will normally lead to a corrective action summary used in order to prevent further incidents.

How Much:

Every incident has an impact representing a very important factor in the data collection process. In many risk assessment processes one of the steps includes the 'Loss Event Profile'. The event is the incident, the loss portion is the attributed dollar loss associated to that event.

- Loss is generally attributed to tangible items (the stolen laptop, the damaged building) but may also be attributed to other losses factors (e.g. reputation loss, loss of intangibles [information], system downtime, etc).
- Incident Loss Tracking may broken down into various criteria:
- Loss Status: Generally categorized as Lost, stolen, or Damaged
- Loss Type: Generally categorized as:
- Direct Loss: The associated direct loss of the item (i.e., the value of the stolen laptop)
  - Indirect Loss: (associated replacement costs such as insurance deductibles or a reputation loss)
  - Cause of Loss: These are similar to Incident 'Why' tracking but one must remember that causes may be related to the entire incident and/or causes related to the loss of individual items. These may be generally described but

again may also be dictated by industry or organizational standards but some samples in various groupings are:

Loss Values:

> In relation to the above factors, the major data collection point is the loss value associated to the event. This will include:
>
> - Loss Per Item: The cost per item lost, stolen, and damaged (including vehicle losses and damages)
> - Total Loss: Total of all items lost, stolen, and damaged in the incident
> - Recovery Values: Represents any recoveries for the incident which may include the actual recovery of an item or, the process (civil recoveries.
> - Net Loss: The loss value after total loss—minus recovery values. These values may be applied per item but MUST be applied to the entire incident.
> - Relation of Loss to the Incident: This important point of loss tracking in response to an incident becomes one of the most important points in the incident management process due to one well known phrase in risk management and risk assessments: Loss Event Profile.

The Loss Event Profile is the matrix of relating the frequency of a type of incident and its associated loss (impact). Without dwelling on the details of the Loss Event Profile, it is safe to say that one cannot attempt to generate this report without first having collected data on the type and frequency of an incident and associated loss values. It is these data collection points that allow us to begin the cross referencing and statistical gathering process needed for risk assessments.

COLLECTION OF DATA

Above we have discussed Incident Reporting is the process of:

- Documenting the Record of events (Who, What, Where, When, Why, How, and How Much) in relation to incidents that occur in relation to an organization.
- We have also laid out some of the generic data points to collect in this process. There are many other data points that may make up your collection program (Incident Disposition, Evidence collection notes, attachments, etc.) but the foundation to support the basics is included above.

The next step is to decide what method of collection can be used. Data entry is generally completed via entry of data into a series of forms, with each form having a series of fields. This process is seen in both annual (paper and pen) and software based systems.

SAMPLE INCIDENT FORM

The following form depicts a multi-page form used to track data within an incident report. The current view shows the tracking of What, When and Where (based on information contained in points 1, 2, and 3 under 'What is Documented' above). Other forms represent other areas for the data collection.

AUTOMATING INCIDENT REPORTING

- While there are many working in the industry that will still not go near a computer and swear by 'I always did it with paper and pen,' there are significant advantages to moving to an automated incident reporting system (software).

- Today, automation and mobile solutions connected to an incident management system allow us anywhere and any time access to the record of events. This also is true of increasing efficiency for data collection where incidents can be recorded in the field by an officer using a mobile device (PDA, Tablet PC etc) instead of having to wait to return to the office to complete the incident.

- *Collaboration:* In addition to mobility, today's 'connected systems' allow for better collaboration. In a world where we need outside divisions, organizations or geographical disperse entities to contribute to our incident reporting and investigations, automated collaborations tools (Microsoft SharePoint, Groove, Live-Link etc) provide a complete and collaborative approach to the incident and investigation process. It is this collaborative approach that provides the full intelligence needed to perform a meaningful risk assessment.

- *Connected Systems:* In many organizations and security divisions, many other processes are now automated (access control, CCTV/DVR, alarms) and controlled by software. These tools are designed to detect events (incidents) and illicit a response. It is natural that we would want these events, detected by other systems, to pass key information (what happened, where and when) to be automatically inputted into the incident management system to complete the entire process and management of incident response.

- In today's world of 'convergence" and XML, integration of systems is common and frequently a requirement of many operation centers.

INCIDENT REPORTING AND STATISTICS

- Incident reporting has one further major requirement after collecting the data: Incident Data Management.
- Incident reporting is not incident data management. Incident Reporting as discussed above is the *collection* of data. Data is essentially nothing unless it is properly managed via process and guidelines and has the ability to be extracted to create accurate quantitative and qualitative results....where data becomes information.
- Accurate historical information about losses or loss events can be among the most useful information kept by an enterprise. First of all, sufficient information permits forecasting of future occurrences......from the science of statistics we know that frequency of occurrence suggests probability of reoccurrence" [1]. [44]
- In many cases, proper incident and loss tracking is an 'Achilles Heel' for many organizations. All organizations face consequences from the occurrence of incidents (both intentional and unintentional) all of which carry an associated loss or impact, but in many cases, recording this information is not done accurately or efficiently which can lead to many associated issues.

Initially, when it comes to generating loss reports, there is often not enough historical or empirical data to garner the necessary data needed to generate Loss Event Profiles or Event Profiles. In many cases, some of the primary issues faced are:

- Data is not Managed: Through uncontrolled ad hoc reporting, the systems or processes in place have not recorded the data accurately so reliance on the report is sometimes questioned.
- Inadequate Systems: In many cases the data cannot be collated properly due to the type of system (5000 paper based reports result in thousands of man hours of work for reporting).
- Lack of Available Data: There is no historical data. Organizations now moving to automated incident management systems only have incidents and historical data based on the inception of the system. So, there may only be a limited amount of records on which to base predictions which again may not be accurate.
- Disparate Systems: Often, organizations will have many disparate systems collecting different data instead of one enterprise level system designed to consolidate data for 'global view'.

44.Walsh, James et al, *Risk Management Manual Vol. 1.* and *POA Publishing 2000. Sec 2 Vulnerability: 2-6.*

Since it is apparent that Incident Reporting and Incident Management are an important part of the risk assessment process and overall security process, why is incident reporting such an Achilles heel? The answer is quite simple....Incident Reporting requires effort.

Generally..no one likes writing reports...not many like reading reports..and it is less likely that people are overly happy when they have to generate annual reports or provide reporting based on stats. Yet, we know we are reliant on the data to complete these actions to get the quantitative and qualitative results we need. Incident management is an overall process combining the data entry vehicle (i.e. an Incident Reporting software package) and the management programs that surround it (incident reporting policies etc).

Commitment to and investment in an incident reporting process can be an organizations best defense in the risk management process. [45] *Incidents* are the reason we need security. If we were able to guarantee that no incidents would ever occur after putting in place a countermeasure, we would not need security. Security is a requirement because there is no guarantee of preventing incidents, only managing the risk associated to an incident occurring.

One of the primary methods we use to identify if a countermeasure is being effective, is to measure if there has been any impact on the asset since deploying the safe guard (in other words, to see if there were any further incidents since deploying the safeguard). If an incident has occurred and a loss suffered, we can now begin to measure the effectiveness of the countermeasure in relation to that incident and decide if further action is required.

In relation to the incident management process, in order to meet the goals of monitor, measure and act, we first need to accurately record data. After this step is where we begin the process of extracting data and statistics.

WHAT TYPES OF STATISTICS AND REPORTS DO WE NEED?

There is no standard set of reports that suits every organization or division; however, most reports will fall into two categories:

- **Standard Reports:** Reports you will generate on a recurring basis. These may be weekly, monthly, quarterly etc. or, specifically defined reports and may combine any combination of metrics (who, what, where, when, why, how and how much). Some examples are but not limited to:

---

45. Denis O'Sullivan, David J. Gibbs. *"The 21st Century Age of 'Insecurity'—Incident Management for Strengthening Homeland Security and Reducing Liability,"* June 2007.

- **Incident/Event Profile**: Produces a report based on # of incidents compared to another metric such as:
  - # of incidents total across organization
  - # of specific incident by type (theft, fraud)
  - # of incidents by multiple types (theft or fraud)
  - # of incidents since or during particular time frames
  - # of incidents at a particular sit
  - # of incidents total across organization plus Loss Information
  - # of specific incident by type (theft, fraud) plus Loss information
  - # of incidents by multiple types (theft or fraud) plus loss information of incidents since or during particular time frames plus Loss information
  - # of incidents at a particular site plus loss information

The event profile is generic. There may be more specific reports that represent a form of the event profile but contain more specific information to gather information in respect to frequency and/or loss information such as; **Incident Frequency Distribution Report**: Produces a report that compares statistics of incident or loss between two periods of time:
- Total number of incidents comparison
- Total Loss Values in dollars
- By Type of Incident
- Date ranges (by Year to Year, Month to Month, Quarter to Quarter, day to day, hour to hour)
- By Location
- By Group

A report like this may be used to compare incident frequency or loss tracking comparing the current month to the last month, or similarly the current year to the last year or any other year.
- **Incident Classification Report**: Produces a detailed report is identifying incidents by specific classifications (theft, fire, fraud etc) and may contain information on location, loss values and date information; however, this report does not contain a span of time comparison. This report would be used where you want to report on totals or identify particular issues. (e.g. thefts occurring in Region 1. etc.).
- **Incident Loss Report**: Produces a report about loss information combining metrics of (Total, Recovered, and Net losses) combined with loss status types (Lost, Stolen,

Damaged as well as Direct, Indirect). This report may also include combinations by site or incident type. This report would be used to identify loss amounts related to other metrics such as generating a report that outlines the total loss and Net loss amounts for all thefts occurring in Region 1

- **Incident Items Report**: Produces a report about specific items involved in incidents and their loss values. This report would be used if you needed to determine loss values in respect to particular item or item types. I.e. All incidents involving laptop thefts where the total loss value is greater than $1000.

- **Incident Yearly/Quarterly/Monthly**: Produces a report providing statistics to date on incident activity (this differs from a frequency distribution in that there is no comparison to another date range). Other metrics may be added such as but not limited to:
  - by incident type (theft, accidents)
  - by group or division
  - by site

- **Outcome – Root Cause Report:** Produces a report based on the cause of an incident (e.g. a report of all incidents at Region 1 where the Cause of incidents were recorded as 'Intentional Failure to Act.'' These standard reports represent only a select few of the reports you may need to generate from your incident management database. The qualifiers are that most reports will always relate to frequency of incidents and loss values. These numbers when accurately recorded provide valuable results in a proactive approach to risk management. There is no standard as to how, who or when these reports are disseminated to but are generally on a periodic basis to management level personnel.

- **Dynamic Query Reports**: On many occasions, standard reports provide us the necessary frequency and loss information based on 'pre-set' criteria'; however, in many scenarios, you may need to generate dynamic queries, or in short, search the database for a particular data set that is not within a standard report. In respect to risk reporting, Dynamic Query Reporting will allow you to data mine further into frequency and loss information by combining a series of data points with other finer points. For example, we may need to determine threat frequencies in general, but when we need to determine threat frequencies in respect to a particular   incident type, during a very specific time period, and a host of other variable metrics.

- **Incident Management & Performance Management**: Incident management is the process of data collection. The concept behind this is to develop a bank of data to turn into actionable intelligence used in our risk programs centered on frequency and loss data. We can however add one more component into the mix: Performance Measurement & Management.

PERFORMANCE MANAGEMENT

Performance measurement is simply measuring against pre-set baselines or targets. For example, if we know over the last four years (based on incident frequency data) that we have had an average of 18 laptop thefts per year, we would not assume that the following year would be reduced to zero. We may likely put programs and countermeasures in place to reduce this number that matches our risk tolerance. So, if we intend that laptop thefts are to be reduced 60 percent for the year, the target benchmark would be roughly eight.

From here, we begin a similar process of Collect, Analyze, and Act: With a benchmark of eight, we will begin to proactively measure based on input data whether we are:

- Within or below the targeted benchmark
- Approaching the benchmark
- Past or exceeded the benchmark

The collection phase falls under incident reporting where each laptop theft is recorded in the database. By proactively monitoring and measuring current values against the benchmark, allows us to identify if our new program or countermeasures are being effective. Our goal is to be within the defined benchmark. If incidents continue to occur impacting our asset and we surpass our benchmark, we know new countermeasures are required, if we are within the benchmark we can assume the countermeasure is working to the level of accepted risk. In short, we are proactively doing Incident Management via Performance Management.

Management is based on ownership. In the Collect, Analyze, Act cycle, the collect and analyze is the measurement. Act is the management where we decide what actions need to take place based on the information we have at hand. Performance management being a proactive approach allows us to:

- Monitor critical business metrics related to incidents
- Be alerted about issues that need attention
- Align actions with strategy
- Act with confidence

METRICS AND MEASURES

In the field of Performance Management in relation to incident management, we tied the measures and metrics.

Measures: What needs to be measured
- by type of incidents
- by sites or locations
- by groups

In the example used above, a combination of measures can be tracked:
- Measure 1: Thefts
- Measure 2: Theft of laptops

In this case, we may measure ALL thefts, or particular types of thefts (of Laptops). Benchmarks would be set for each. These represent the measure.

Metrics: What will be used as analysis to measure. Number of incidents:
- Year to Date
- Running Total

Loss Information
- Year to date
- Running total

To tie all of this together using the above sample, we would be measuring Laptop Thefts with target benchmarks of:
- Number of Incidents: Target 8
- Losses: Total $18,000

Based on year to date and running totals. As we add incidents to the system, our performance management (Actions) is based on our relative position to these key performance indicators.

QUALITATIVE V. QUANTITATIVE

In various parts of the sections above, we have mentioned and discussed quantitative and qualitative results. Simply, qualitative being the 'picture' and quantitative being the statistical fact supporting the picture. In many cases we see this as graphs in bar, pie, line and other charts that allow us to quickly depict both good and problem areas by quickly looking at the picture, which we usually then follow-up by looking at the actual numbers supporting the chart or report we have produced.

   For example, Chart #1 (shown at the conclusion of this chapter) depicts incident frequency over a span of four years. Qualitatively we can see a decrease based on the length of the bars and see that 2002 was the worst year. Quantitatively we can then look at the supporting numbers along the bottom of the chart.

In Charts #2 and #3 (illustrated at the conclusion of this chapter), qualitatively we can see which building had the most incidents and which was the most frequent category of incidents. These are each supported by the qualitative statistics.

This approach is used in many facets of what is done in reporting. Other known and common approaches can also be applied such as the standard performance measures charting Red, Yellow, and Green (see charts at conclusion of chapter).

In our world, these common colors represent identifying signals no matter how they are applied, whether it's in a traffic light, a bomb blast chart or a performance chart, the colors are indicative of:

- Green = Good
- Yellow = Approaching Not so Good
- Red = Not Good

Applying these foundations to Performance Measurement and incident reporting, these color codes allow us to pro-actively measure on a qualitative and quantitative approach where we are in respect to our key performance indicators via metrics tree reporting:

In metrics tree reporting (one style of Performance reporting); a top down approach is used to 'drill down' through measures. The benefit of metrics tree reporting and the point of this sample, is to illustrate how we can easily and proactively determine issue areas.

In these samples below, each box represents a measure based on type of incident measured by:

- Location (Site)
- Actual Incident Data Year to Date
- Target (set benchmark)

ASSAULT Site 1		ASSAULT Site 2		ASSAULT Site 3	
Actual	25	Actual	18	Actual	21
Target	21	Target	25	Target	25

Below, the metrics tree shows a variety of measures based on incident type and their relative color coding based on their benchmarks and various metric types.

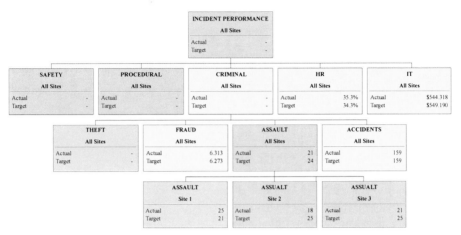

SUMMARY

Statistics and incident reporting clearly go hand in hand. We have demonstrated that without sufficient incident reporting and incident management, the ability to generate effective frequency and loss reports cannot be considered accurate or reliable. Commitment to an effective incident reporting and management plan will lead to effective and assist with developing a reliable risk assessment analysis.

Extracting the Terms

Given the concepts above relating to incident management, it becomes apparent that some of the common terms used in the risk management reporting process are dependent on good incident management. For example:

- **Event**: The incident that will occur via human based or natural based occurrences.

- **Impact:** the measured effect on the organization from the event. Also referred to as the *consequence* relative to the dollar loss.

- **Loss:** the resulting impact from each event usually measured in dollars (but may be other loss factor)

- **Frequency**: how many times the event has occurred over a span of time. This may be known as likelihood or probability

- **Single Loss Expectancy**: Determine the loss value from a single event.

- **Annual Loss Expectancy**: Determining Annual Loss using metrics of: # of times event is likely to occur X Single Loss Expectancy per event.

- **Threat:** The event that can occur

- **Risk**: "The <u>likelihood</u> of damage or loss multiplied by the potential magnitude of the loss"

No matter what risk assessment paradigm is used, all of them have similar frameworks and most have one particular common element: Generating event profiles and loss event profiles, all which start with a basic foundation in incident management principles.

Most first attempts to introduce loss reporting and incident management to an organization is met with resistance by senior management and IT departments. Corporate security views this as being "over their heads" or capable of demonstrating a weakness in the existing security program. These perceptions are entirely incorrect. It is difficult to assure those who are reluctant, but the following outline may help mitigate initial reticence:

- At first glance, incident reporting and management programs appear to be labor intensive and complicated. They are not. It is much like a database program used for accounting (small business or home). Once the construction of the accounts, data entry flow, and report criteria are implemented, operation of the system becomes second nature. It is far more transparent than many programs staff are already using (e.g., spread sheets, word processing, etc.).

- When you examine the types of data that are generated and the significant support it provides to a risk assessment process, reticence will dissolve. Reports generated will add an entirely new clarity to understanding risk and how it is or is not being affected by your security program.

- When senior management becomes aware of the types of reports loss reporting and incident management systems produce, they will view corporate security from an entirely different perspective. Review of these data and reports will assist in demonstrating the net present value of security versus old perceptions of security being a cost center.

CHART #1

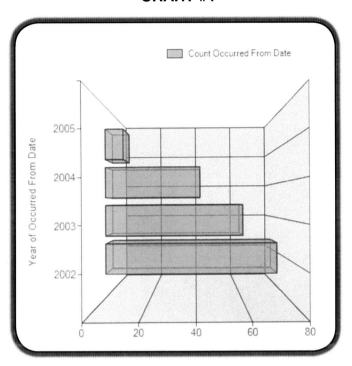

CHART #2

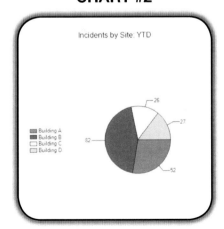

CHART #3

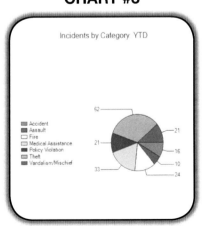

## CHAPTER SEVEN

Demographic Analysis in Risk Assessment

A wide variety of risk assessment techniques have been discussed in prior chapters. In this chapter we examine a specific kind of risk assessment perspective: demographic and neighborhood characteristics as they relate to crime risk. In this context, we are really talking about the chances that potential criminal offenders may attempt to steal, damage or injure a target, be it a thing or a person, as a function of neighborhood and demographic characteristics.

Being social communities, neighborhoods and their demographic components, in an analytical sense, can be viewed as complicated combinations of many variables and characteristics—some measurable and some not. Therefore, the task of converting local (neighborhood) demographics into useful risk assessment metrics is also complicated requiring multivariate, data analytic approaches of some sophistication if one desires to produce valid and reliable risk assessments.

The purpose here is not to uncover the causes of criminal behavior (the interest of the criminologist) but to outline a methodology which would provide the security or risk manager a tool for anticipating where, in a geographic sense, crimes relevant for that manager's duties might be more or less foreseeable. The problem that security managers face is the protection of a variety of assets not the amelioration of society's ills. To that end, crime control resources need to be focused proportionately in relation to the risk of these crime-related losses.

We suggest that an analysis of the ecology of an area (the interplay between people and place) is an essential piece of any thorough risk assessment. Thus in this chapter we shall present a:

- brief discussion of the literature examining the relationships existent among neighborhood and demographic characteristics and crime, short discussion of the multivariate perspective and analysis procedures, and

- risk assessment methodology with examples based upon these discussions.

PERSPECTIVES ON CRIME CAUSATION

Criminologists have studied a wide variety of perspectives in their quest to uncover the causes of crime and develop remedies to prevent criminal activity. These approaches have addressed:

- Ecological factors focusing on the neighborhood and the extent of its "disorganization,"

- Biological factors including biochemistry (including drug use), heredity, brain dysfunctions and many other "organism"—based causes of criminal conduct,
- Psychological factors including intelligence, various behavioral pathologies and so on,
- Socialization or "strain" and "control" factors which involve stress on the individual and the breakdown of the bonds to society which keep one from violating the law,
- Power, conflict and labeling factors which develop from power relationships that enable some groups to define criminal activity and deny access to other groups to power and wealth,
- Perspectives having to do with a variety of ideological positions regarding the definitions of legally acceptable behavior and a variety of other less studied areas.

While all of these approaches have some relevance to crime risk assessment and deterrence to a greater or lesser degree, most of them have little direct application to the practice of risk assessment of the type addressed in this chapter.

For example, biological and psychological factors are relevant for risk assessments on the individual level where such concerns are part of job-related activities. Socialization, power, conflict and labeling factors have implications for policy making and intervention strategies, but not for crime risk assessments and so on.

On the other hand, the analyses of ecological factors relating population variables (demography) and neighborhood characteristics to behavior—in this case, delinquent and criminal behavior, have a direct application to risk assessments appropriate for security and risk managers because these are measures reflecting the **crime potentials of places rather than of individuals**. Specifically, the ecological perspective as it relates to criminal activity addresses the extent to which members of a community are and feel bound together. The less a community is able to maintain its environment the less it is able to maintain collective ties that enable its members to exert social control and minimize criminal behavior. Conversely, the more a community is able to sustain itself and maintain its physical structure the more likely it will be able to develop and maintain social control of the type which will minimize the kinds of activities that are interest to the security profession.

At this point the reader may point out that this argument applies only to those behaviors that are deemed appropriate or inappropriate by the particular community under discussion and consideration. In fact, that is true. Members of well-supported and maintained communities may be able to promulgate their values and exert control over their members more effectively than are members of less "fortunate" communities, areas or neighborhoods; but that does not imply that crime cannot occur in these better-endowed areas as well. In fact, crimes are committed by individuals from these areas as well, but the criminal acts tend to be of a different type.

The reality is that no, crime causation perspective explains all criminal activity. The further one digs into the study of human behavior the more one finds that all of these theories interface at one point or another. Violent offenders and thieves can come from wealthy areas as well as from the lower income neighborhoods.

Corporate criminals are much more likely to live in areas considered to be "low" in crime, although a corporate criminal may do more harm and cause greater social costs than a "street" criminal. This kind of thinking has led many criminologists to argue that crime is socially- defined by those in power and that all criminal activity essentially reflects sets of definitions, not "real" criminality.

This argument ultimately takes one to a conclusion that whether or not an act should be considered criminal depends upon your point of view/ideology. Thus, the offender who robs a gas station may be outraged by the oil company CEO who fixes the books to maximize stock value causing thousands of investors and pensioners to lose their savings when the whole scam crumbles, while that same corporate executive is similarly outraged when one of his stations is robbed. The same kind of definitional issues surround the commission of political crimes—crimes committed by those in power to further their personal or political ends through the exercise of their power positions in society.

One should, therefore, understand from this example, that the appropriate choice of a risk assessment methodology depends upon the kind of risk one is attempting to estimate.

In this chapter we are interested in assessing the risks of crimes more commonly defined as "street" crimes and/or crimes committed by individuals or groups of individuals directly against persons or property that directly or indirectly also impacts the security within their facility.

ECOLOGY, DEMOGRAPHY, AND CRIME

From this momentary but necessary diversion into the world of criminological thinking let us now look more directly at the value and strength of the ecological perspective. This line of thinking had its origins at the University of Chicago in the 1920s and, therefore, it has been called the "Chicago School of Thought" although modern researchers have taken this study far beyond that early but profoundly influential work. In short, this theoretical perspective states that the more a community is socially disorganized the greater the potential for criminal activity. The theory has several components that attempt to explain the causal and associative dynamics of the elements of social disorganization as they relate to crime and delinquency. These components include the psychological implications of community and neighborhood, the genesis of gang behavior, the development of delinquent subcultures, subcultural phenomena and cultural transmission and a whole field research methodological regimen. The reader is referred to the references at the end of this chapter for representative citations for these aspects of this perspective. However, of particular note for our purposes here was the postulating of the "Concentric Zone Theory" which looked at Chicago as a series of five zones, each of which typifying a particular ecological character. Thus, the inner city was the business district. The next zone out from the center was labeled "transitional" in that it was composed of factories, deteriorated housing, dilapidated buildings and immigrants. Working class housing surrounded this transitional area which was then surrounded by the residential or single-family zone. The suburban zone lay in the outer zone or the hinterland of the city. Being the first crime mapping group, Chicago researchers overlaid criminal and gang activities on the city map and found that the "transitional" zone experienced the highest amount of delinquent activity and also displayed, by their definition, the highest amount of social disorganization or lowest amount of "social control." This low control-high crime area persisted through time independent, for the most part, of the ethnicity of its occupants. The researchers posited that a criminal subculture develops in areas like this that persists over time and place even as the population shifts and moves. This transitional zone was characterized by:

- Poverty
- Deteriorated housing
- Residential mobility
- Ethnic heterogeneity
- Lack of shared value system
- Inability to maintain social control
- Resulting social disorganization

As these and other related factors come together in a social area, the likelihood of crime increases.

Recent Work in the Ecology of Crime

Over the last thirty years the research begun by the Chicago School has blossomed into a highly refined research agenda producing some of the most powerful empirical work in criminological studies. This work has emphasized and reasserted the importance of "place" in the production of and influence on human behavior - particularly criminal behavior. Felson and Cohen in "Human ecology and crime: A routine activity approach," state:

"Prior explanations of the distributions of crime have tended to emphasize the criminal intentions of people without considering adequately the circumstances in which criminal acts occur. This paper examines how community structure generates these circumstances and applies Amos Hawley's human ecological theory in treating criminal acts..."

Oscar Newman building on the work of C. Ray Jeffery in his seminal work, **Defensible Space: Crime Prevention Through Urban Design,** showed how the design of the environment can affect levels of criminal activity.

Wilson and Kelly writing in **The Atlantic Monthly** ("Broken Windows – The police and neighborhood safety") in 1982 argued persuasively that neighborhood deterioration tends to feed further decay and produce crime. Robert Sampson et.al. reported in **Science** in 1997 ("Neighborhoods and Violent Crime: A Multilevel Study of Collective Efficacy,") that:

"It is hypothesized that collective efficacy, defined as social cohesion among neighbors, combines with their willingness to intervene on behalf of the common good, is linked to reduced violence....Multilevel analyses showed that a measure of collective efficacy yields high between-neighborhood reliability and is negatively associated with variations in violence, when individual-level characteristics, measurement error and prior violence are controlled."

The authors also concluded that the level of collective efficacy was strongly influenced by the level of poverty and neighborhood migration – a measure of stability.

The most recent report on this topic by the National Institute of Justice (2007), *"Adolescents, Neighborhoods, and Violence: Recent Findings from the Project on Human Development in Chicago Neighborhoods,"* concluded:

"The body of research reviewed in the articles generally concludes that neighborhood conditions and social processes are important predictors of violence ***beyond*** *(emphasis added) the attributes of individual residents themselves."*

Conclusion Regarding Ecological and Demographic Conditions and Crime

The literature is extensive and definitive in supporting the notion that the neighborhood (place) is a major contributor to predicting where crime and violence are likely to occur. Poverty acts through the neighborhood by limiting the ability of the inhabitants of an area to affect and control their lives in any substantive manner. That inability manifests itself in a variety of observable characteristics of the neighborhood such as:

- Deteriorated housing stock
- Overcrowded housing
- Poorly maintained or missing sanitary and heating equipment
- Unkempt properties and streets
- Lack of home ownership, and of the population demographic characteristics such as:
- Low income
- Low educational levels
- High proportion of unmarried heads of households with children
- High population turnover or mobility, and of the social interaction patterns such as:
- Lack of neighborhood social control and order resulting in
- Social disorganization and
- High crime and violence rates.

The issue now is how do we take this theoretical perspective with all of its empirical support and place it into a workable paradigm to produce a useful crime risk assessment?

THE MULTIVARIATE PERSPECTIVE AND CRIME RISK ASSESSMENT

As should be obvious from the above discussion, the assessment of crime risk requires the joint consideration of many variables covering a variety of demographic and neighborhood factors. That complex analysis requires the use of multivariate modeling and data analytic techniques. First, we need to build a model or "construct" of these relationships so that we can specify the necessary measurement variables and their relationships to each other and the potential for crime in a given area. Figure 1 below suggests a workable multivariate model, which relates a series of measurable variables on the left side of the figure:

- Population information (demographics)
- Housing Data (neighborhood conditions)
- Mobility (neighborhood stability)
- Economic data (ability to affect the environment), and
- Education data (ability to produce wealth and affect the environment) to the concept

of "social disorganization"—the circle in the left of the middle of the model. These variables are indicators of the concept of social disorganization.

The analysis does not actually measure social disorganization; it is inferred from the theory and the variables. Of course, social disorganization in this model relates to crime but as the arrows indicate, crime also contributes to social disorganization. Thus these two concepts are mutually causative in this model. On the right side of the model we see a set of indicators of crime:

- Crime loss reports from businesses
- Victim reports of crimes they have experienced
- Police reports of crimes in an area, and
- Self-reports of crimes interviewees have said they committed.

As with social disorganization, we are inferring the concept of crime from measurements of these variables that we hypothesized are indicators of crime.

FIGURE 1. A MULTIVARIATE MODEL CRIME RISK ASSESSMENT

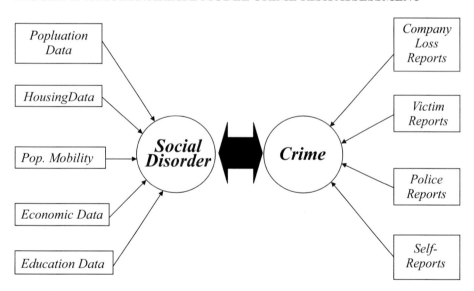

Now all we need is a methodology capable of analyzing all of these variables together and enough data from enough locations to build a model to produce estimates of the magnitude of these relationships and assess the ability of the variables on the left side of the model to predict the magnitude of the variables on the right side. Then we shall be able to estimate crime potentials from social disorganization measures by location or neighborhood.

MULTIVARIATE DATA ANALYSIS

The techniques which best allow the examination of the relationships among a set of variables are subsumed under the general rubric of "multiple regression analysis.

"Multiple regression analysis includes a wide range of analytical techniques that generate estimation equations of the relationships, which exit among sets of variables both to each other and as predictors of one another. Many complex issues arise from this kind of approach but suffice to say here that, properly applied, relationships and predictive power can be determined and developed which would not be possible by any other methodology.

Essentially, multiple regression relates a series of predictor variables, the "X's" in the equation below, weighted by the "b's" (beta weights) with "p" being the number of variables, to a dependent variable, "Y", in this case in a linear fashion. Further, this simple model can be expanded to include more than one "Y" or dependent variable and also to account for nonlinear relationships as well. $Y = a + b_1 * X_1 + b_2 * X_2 + ... + b_p * X_p$

By gathering data for both sides of the model across a variety locations and neighborhoods, and plugging those data into a statistical routine designed to produce the best fit among all of these data, we shall then be able to estimate crime levels of neighborhoods by entering the variables which relate to the concept of social disorganization. The extent to which the predictions accurately relate one side of the model to the other determines the validity of the model.

This model is the basis for demographically and ecologically –based crime risk assessments for a variety of geographical areas such as blocks or groups of blocks in a city, census tract, ZIP code, police districts or beats or any other relevant geographical area.

We shall now display the results of the application of a model of this type for three different cities in the U.S.: Washington, D.C., San Francisco, and Philadelphia.

Model Applications

To demonstrate the flexibility of this modeling perspective the Figures display crime risk maps by both crimes against persons and property for several geographic boundaries:

- Census Tracts

- Police Districts

- ZIP Codes and Neighborhood Designations

In the following maps we have designated crime risks by both a numerical score and a color. The numerical score is derived from the equation and model described above and ranges from 1 to 2000, where 1 is the lowest crime risk score and 2000 the highest. We have normalized the scores against the average for the United States which we have given the value of 100. Thus a 200 would be a crime risk that is twice the U.S. average and 50 would be on-half and so on.

To each range of scores we have given a color to designate the crime risk as follows. If the crime risk score ranges from:

- 1 to 99, the color is green,
- 100 to 199, the color is yellow,
- 200 to 399 dark yellow or light pink depending on the map,
- 400 to 799, darker pink and,
- 800 and above, red.

Washington, D.C.

Figure 2 for Washington, D.C., shows the crime risk scores as displayed by census tract ranging from 21 to 2000 and for tract crime risk color from green to red. Thus, the D.C. area encompasses a wide range of crime risks.

In Figure 3 these crime risk categories are overlaid by actual crime incident data reported to the police. If the crime risk model is doing a good job of estimating the actual crime experience data, the density of the police incident data should become greater as the crime risk color becomes redder.

In fact, such is the case with the D.C. data. The green areas show little or no police activity, while the red areas display very high levels of police activity and the tallow and pin areas lie more or less in between.

The fit between forecasted and actual police will not be perfect for several reasons:

- no model is absolutely perfect,
- human behavior is not completely predictable,
- the model predicts the "potential" for criminal activity not the certainty:
- security and police measures can affect criminal behavior in an area,
- micro- level situational circumstances can affect behavior realizations,
- police data have variable levels of validity and reliability,
- demographic predictor variables have similar validity and reliability levels,

- other unmeasured factors may impinge upon the predictive validity and behavioral outcomes in particular areas.

Nonetheless, the overlay of police data on tract level model risk levels shows that the high crime potential areas produce large numbers of reported police incidents while the low risk areas do not display much police activity.

FIGURE 2. CRIME RISKS BY CENSUS TRACT: WASHINGTON, DC.

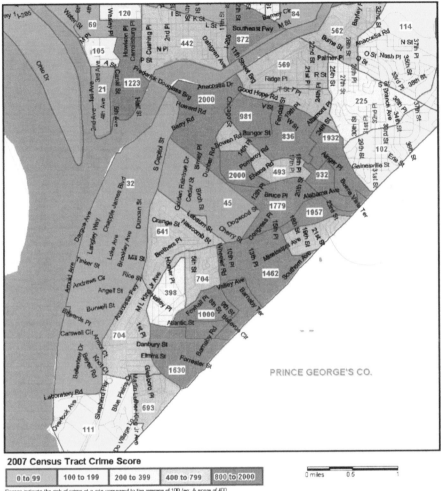

2007 Census Tract Crime Score

0 to 99	100 to 199	200 to 399	400 to 799	800 to 2000

Scores indicate the risk of crime at a site compared to the average of 100 (eg. A score of 400 means that the risk is 4 times the average and a score of 50 means the risk is half the average)

0 miles   0.5   1

FIGURE 3. CENSUS TRACT CRIME SCORE

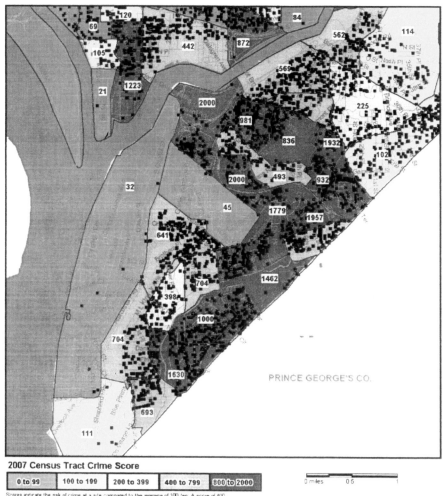

FIGURE 4. SAN FRANCISCO

YEAR 2000 RATIO OF PERSONAL CRIME REPORTS TO U.S. AVERAGE

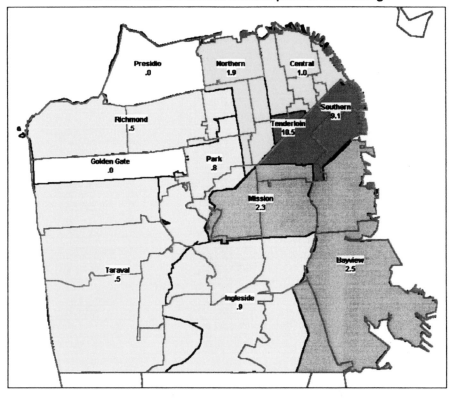

FIGURE 5. SAN FRANCISCO

YEAR 2000 RATIO OF PROPERTY CRIME REPORTS TO U.S. AVERAGE

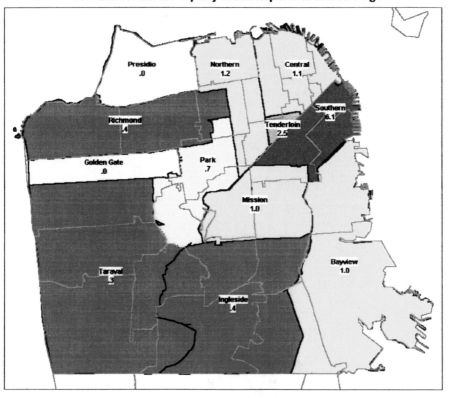

San Francisco
Year 2000 Ratio of Property Crime Reports to U.S. Average

FIGURE 6. PROPERTY CRIME RISKS BY POLICE DISTRICT: PHILADELPHIA, PA

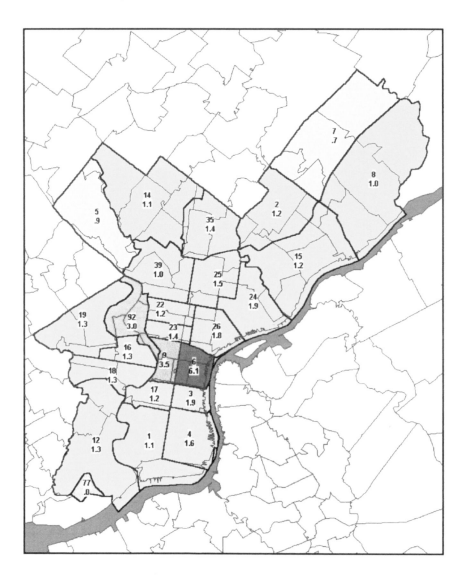

Summary and Conclusion

In this chapter we considered a variety of crime causation theories and perspectives ranging from emphasis on individual biological and psychological factors to larger societal orientations and concluded that the ecological/demographic perspective offers the most useful application potential for practitioners working in the crime risk assessment environment. This ecological approach has a long history of theory and research attention in the fields of criminology and criminal justice, including major recent empirical validations which assert that neighborhood factors may be the most relevant for identifying the loci of criminal activity and for targeting prevention and control interventions. With that persuasive evidence in mind, we then suggested that demographic and neighborhood factors could be conceptualized in such a way to produce a viable model for identifying and ranking crime risks by specific geographic locations. The results of a model were then presented in map form and validated using several different data sources and formats to show the predictive robustness and such a model. We then concluded that ecological modeling could produce valid and reliable risk estimates for security and risk managers to aid in their production of crime risk assessments for loss prediction and control. This approach provides one useful tool in the practice of the art and science of crime in a risk assessment.

## CHAPTER EIGHT

Internal and Human Factor Controls

For risk assessments to be effective on an ongoing basis, adaptability is necessary to keep pace with the labile nature of risk and the strategies developed to respond to same.

Risks are becoming more difficult to identify. Even more challenging for most organizations is applying the results of an ongoing risk assessment strategy and implementing effective internal controls that include new and updated risk strategies. Risk mitigation techniques and human factor controls that will help guide all appropriate individuals are critical to making better decisions.

Unfortunately many organizations and third-party professional services focus their risk assessment efforts toward beating or meeting audit requirements rather than identifying real-life risks, mitigating risks, and implementing and managing their ongoing mitigation strategies. Incident reporting and incident tracking are a good examples of compliance challenges.

Findings

Careful analysis of recent incidents, breaches, lawsuits, failures, attacks and embarrassing headlines clearly indicate that organizational leaders are not implementing lessons learned into their internal controls framework at the organizational level or communicating internal controls at the individual-level. In other words the incidents and failures that other organizations are experiencing demonstrate that similar risks and failures are occurring over and over again and that defensive strategies to deter, delay, deny and/or respond to known risks are not being implemented by a control strategy. It only takes one poor decision by one individual to cause a serious, expensive and embarrassing incident. And while it may take years and years to build a reputation… it only takes one individual's bad decision to ruin it.

While focused on the importance of individual-level awareness and accountability 60 percent of all information security and information incidents are due to *human* factors.

INTERNAL CONTROLS AND HUMAN FACTORS

Internal controls are put in place to keep the organization on course towards profitability, stability, and survivability, as well as enabling management to deal with changing strategies, competitive environments, customer trust and future success. Internal controls promote efficiency, reduce risks of asset loss and help ensure compliance with laws and regulations.

Human factors include any decisions an individual makes or should make to ensure your organization's internal controls and risk mitigation strategies are 'connected' with day-to-day operations for all individuals.

Human factors include individual-level decisions that need to be made to deter, delay, deny and/or respond to risks encountered while at work or when individuals are handling work related assets and information while away from the office or at home. Human factors include individual-level decisions involving Risk Management, Compliance, Legal Due Diligence, Employment, Emergency Management, Information Technology, Information Handling, Incident Reporting, and many other business loss potentials.

Human factors guidelines and internal controls must be clearly communicated to employees, vendors, contractors, partners, service providers, etc., to ensure good decisions and risk mitigation strategies that are part of the culture across multiple departments and locations.

COMMUNICATIONS AND RISK ASSESSMENT METRICS

How do improved communications at the individual-level improve risk management efforts across the entire organization?

How can individual-level awareness and accountability of internal controls improve risk assessment metrics and help measure effectiveness of risk strategies?

How can internal controls and awareness help identify new risk strategies and new threats on the horizon?

Many organization leaders are looking for new technological solutions that could become their 'silver bullet' for risk assessments and risk management, however technology solutions are most effective in dealing with technical controls and not with internal controls and human factors.

Improving communications and clarity of risk assessment metrics for the most part have been limited to technology; including systems, networks, servers, databases, physical security, etc. We are learning the importance of risk assessment metrics with internal controls and human factors as incidents continue to mount and as new regulations are forcing management at all levels to better understand metrics for internal controls as well proactive and reactive controls. What methodology should we use to provide metrics that identify the success or failure of our risk mitigation strategies?

PHASES - RISK ASSESSMENTS AND INTERNAL CONTROLS

Risk assessment phases include:
- Identify Risks
- Measure and Assess the Risks
- Control the Risks
- Monitor the Risks

Organization leaders must implement, manage and monitor their risk management processes as well as their internal controls, technical controls, reactive and proactive efforts on an ongoing basis. Just as risk assessment metrics are important, ongoing risk management metrics are critical to ensure the organization is aware of efficiencies, performance levels, risks, threats, situational awareness, culture and controls are connected with day-to-day operations.

Internal controls and human factors phases include:

- Prepare – where organization leaders must develop and communicate the importance of creating and maintaining

Culture of Preparedness

- Prevent – where organization leaders must communicate to all individuals what needs to be prevented and prevention is critical.
- Respond – where organization leaders must define clear roles and responsibilities for individuals to take in response to different types of situations and incidents and realize that alerting systems (e.g. announcements) will still result in chaos and panic if individuals are not prepared, aware and accountable for their roles and responsibilities.
- Recover – where organization leaders must use imagination and ask "then what?" for each risk and each situation to ensure that individuals clearly understand where, what, when and how their organization will recover from different situations, risks and threats.

EXAMPLES OF TECHNICAL AND HUMAN FACTOR CONTROLS

Organizations quickly learned the importance of anti-virus and spyware software and how a multi-level configuration can be a more effective strategy in preventing risks and threats to their information. Anti-virus and spyware software can be more effective when implemented on centrally located gateway servers, individual servers, individual PCs, individual laptops, individual mobile devices and etc.

- Anti-virus and spyware software must be *updated* on an ongoing basis or new risks and threats will not be identified and prevented. Anti-virus and spyware software also provides metrics in the form of signature file updates that can be easily *monitored* to ensure the latest software updates are in place. Like anti-virus and spyware, internal controls and Human Factors tools can be more effective when situational awareness is 'implemented, updated and monitored' at the individual-level. New specialized tools like MOAT (Managed Ongoing Awareness and Trust) enable an organization's management to implement, update, and monitor internal controls frameworks and Human Factors challenges.

For example, when internal controls and Human Factor tools are being utilized and an organization has new or updated internal controls (policies, procedures, plans, roles, responsibilities, guidelines, strategies, etc.) management can easily update or create a new document, highlight critical information, assign it to the appropriate groups or individuals, and notify the appropriate groups and individuals that a new or updated document requires their review and acknowledgment.

Once an individual has received their notification, then can login to the secured Internet accessible site and access those documents that apply to them and acknowledge the new situational awareness as well as roles and responsibilities. The individual acknowledgements are tracked and documented by the internal controls tools to provide important metrics and time-stamped audit trail reports on demand. Individuals and management can access their assigned documents and updates anytime and anywhere Internet access is available.

Feedback is critical and providing individuals with clear instructions, procedures and contact lists for questions and feedback regarding the new or updated documents will make incident reporting much more effective and efficient. Unfortunately, many 'red flags' have gone unreported because individuals did not know how to give feedback or take proactive actions or how to 'connect the dots'.

Management can access and download on-demand reports and metrics measuring individual-level compliance and awareness. More comprehensive internal controls tools track and document individual-level activity and can send automatic reminders or allow management to manually monitor which individuals have or have not acknowledged their assigned documents to ensure a culture of awareness.

Most organizations would never consider operating their business without anti-virus and spyware software due to the risks and threats and damage that can be caused. However, now that 60 percent of security and privacy incidents are due to Human

Factors and lack of awareness of internal controls, why would any organization choose to operate their business without internal controls tools?

An organization can have the best 'technology products' AND an organization can have 'policies, procedures and plans developed' AND an organization can have the best 'incident reporting forms' AND the best 'defensive strategies', BUT WITHOUT INDIVIDUAL-LEVEL AWARENESS and ACCOUNTABILITY the organization will be unable:

- To have access to all needed forms
- To have clear understanding of strategies developed in response to foreseeable risks

So having said that, specialized software enables and empowers an organization's management [top-down] to ensure situational awareness and accountability at the individual-level [bottom-up] with a direct effect on the bottom line.

SPECIALIZED WEB-BASED SOFTWARE "TOOLS" ENSURE

- That all loss reports ARE reported because that is a Human Control Factor.
- That management can provide clear details on **What** the report is, **How** to report, and **When** to report all details.
- Ensure that individuals have "acknowledged" their responsibility for incident reporting.
- Ensure "CYA's" for management to demonstrate due diligence that the organization's management has clearly communicated the proper details and that individual People have acknowledged their awareness and accountability for reporting.
- Compares the defensive strategies employed with the ongoing incidents to see if strategies are mitigating exposure to risks.

Specialized wen-based software enables an organization's management and security management team to review defensive strategies in "REAL TIME" and to update defensive strategies in "REAL TIME" and to communicate new and updated defensive strategies in "REAL TIME" to ALL appropriate individuals. If individuals are not aware of updated defensive strategies and risk mitigation strategies, then people cannot take proactive actions and cannot make good decisions.

Specialized Web-based software identifies <u>new</u> risks that may be on the horizon:

- Specialized Web-based software enables an organization's management to communicate and ensure that new information, new policies, new defense strategies, new best practices and new guidelines are implemented and acknowledged by all appropriate individuals. This defines the data that is needed for "metrics" that tracks and quantifies the productivity of security strategies and the "net present value" of a security program investment.

- Personnel using specialized Web-based software will continue to learn about new risks on the horizon and ensure PEOPLE make the necessary changes in configurations, incident reporting, proactive decisions, and reactive decisions.;
- Specialized Web-based software makes sure top-down and bottom-up efforts are coordinated, tracked, documented, archived and maintained on an ongoing basis.

WHEN INTERNAL CONTROLS ARE ALIGNED

Connecting-the-dots and measurability are key components to ensure that risk assessments will result in performance improvements.

Organizations that do not connect-the-dots and align risk assessments with internal controls and individual-level awareness often find themselves in the headlines or facing serious fines and lawsuits.

Clear precedents have been established through FTC settlements with multiple organizations that have resulted in organizations having to implement risk assessment programs and comprehensive internal controls.

Improving risk assessments and internal controls and individual-level awareness and accountability even a little can bring big gains. Regularly scheduled management meetings to review risk assessment reports and strategies, reports tracking the progress of internal controls being developed and reports tracking how strategies and internal controls are being communicated and acknowledged by individuals will help management better understand risks and threats as well as preparing and planning for the future.

Lastly, aligning risk assessments with internal controls and human factors will build a 'culture of trust'. In today's constantly changing environments, building trust starts with accountability and practicing accountability builds trust. The best accountability is where people hold themselves accountable against the standards and internal controls that are mutually agreed upon. Accountability will build trust and confidence and with this trust and confidence an organization's management can make serious improvements within their security management program.

Commentary

This text was written to introduce students, business, and security professionals to an important paradigm, *Security Risk Assessment*. Too often Security Risk Assessment is confused with *Risk Management*. For anyone delegated with the responsibility of *asset protection*, I trust this text was of value. When I started this project, I was immediately struck by the limited body of knowledge that was available; particularly a text that could be useful to business students and business professionals.

With over 45 years of security management experience, I am constantly amazed at the number of organizations who begin integrating defensive security strategies without knowing what threats their security strategies should deter, detect, or respond to. Certainly more than one text needs to be written as some organizations have very unique and high level vulnerabilities that the methodologies outlined in this text will not adequately address. I would urge persons with asset protection responsibility to view this text as a primer and seek additional data as they deem necessary. There simply is no panacea in identifying and responding to foreseeable security risks in every organization, but a serious effort must be made before security strategies are implemented. To assist with your research in developing your risks assessment program, the following references are offered:

__A White Paper on a Value-Added Model for Security Management__, Stephen Gale, Keith Duncan, Rudolph Yaksick, John Tofflemire, Research Supported by the American Society for Industrial Security Foundation (ASIS), December, 1990.

__Assessing the Terrorist__ Threat, Security Technology & Design (Magazine), John Fay, August, 2004.

__Assessing the Terrorist Threat__, Security Technology & Design (Magazine), John Fay, August, 2004.

__Beyond Fear__, Thinking Sensibly About Security in an Uncertain World, Risk Assessment and Site Selection, Stephen G. Ward, BAI.

__Business Risk Assessment__, The Institute of Internal Auditors, David McNamee, CIA, CISA, SFE, CGFM, FIIA(M), August, 1999.

__Crime Prevention Through Environmental Design__, An Operational Handbook, National Institute of Justice, Research Report, December, 1984.

Crossing Corporate Turf, Gerald W. Wernz and Timothy L. Williams, 1994.

Effective Security Management, Charles A. Sennewald, Butterworth-Heinemann, Fourth Edition, Chapter 17, pp. 196.

General Security Risk Assessment, Guideline, Page 5, ASIS International, 2003.

Guide for Premises Security, 2005 Edition, NFPA 730, Peter D. Blauvelt, January, 2004.

Handbook of Loss Prevention and Crime Prevention, Lawrence J. Fennelly, Butterworths, Second Edition, Chapter 3, p. 37, Copyright 1989.

http://travel.state.gov/visa/americans/americans_1252.html

http://www.gao.gov/special.pubs/ai00033.pdf

http://www.networkcomputing.com/1121/1121f3.html

Information Security Risk Assessment - Practices of Leading Organizations, U.S. Government Accounting Office (GAO), 11/99.

Introduction to Risk Analysis, 2003, C & A Security Risk Analysis Group **(www. security-risk-analysis.com/introduction.htm).**

Quantitative Terrorism Risk Assessment, Dr. Gordon Foo, Risk Management Solutions, Ltd.
http://www.weatherdesk.net/NewsPress/Quantitative_Terrorism_Risk_Assessment.pdf

Rick Assessment and Security Program Design, Ira Somerson, January, 1995.

Risk Management for Security Professionals, Carl A. Roper, Butterworth-Heinemann, Chapter 4, pp. 34-35, Copyright, 1999.

Risk Assessment Survey Form, Fleet Financial Security, David R. Struckhoff, Ph.D, December, 2001.

Risk Assessment and Site Selection, Stephen G. Ward, BAI.

Risk Analysis Without Pain, Carol R. Hamilton, President, Expert Systems Software, ISPNews, January/February, 1992.

Risk Management for Security Professionals, Carl A. Roper, Butterworth Heinemann, Chapter 3, pp. 20-21, Copyright 1999.

Security Survey and Risk Assessment, Department of Education (UK) of An Roinn Oideachais (from Internet), 1/06

Security Systems: Upgrades and Retrofits, Randy Dunn, Today's Facility Manager, 1/01

Security Consulting, Charles A. Sennewald, CPP, Second Edition, Butterworth-Heinemann, 1996.

Security Systems: Upgrades and Retrofits, Randy Dunn, Today's Facility Manager, 1/01

Special Event Security Management, Loss Prevention and Emergency Service, Chapter 2, pp.11-12, Alexander Berlonghi, M.S., Bookmasters, Inc., 1996.

The Alliance for Enterprise Security Risk Management, Convergence of Enterprise Security Organizations, Booz/Allen/Hamilton, November 8, 2005.

The Security/Safety Merger, *Security World Magazine (Cahners Publishing), Arthur E. Torrington, January, 1975 (Part I).*

The Alliance for Enterprise Security Risk Management, Convergence of Enterprise Security Organization, Section 3.1, p. 6, Booz/Allen/Hamilton, November 8, 2005.

Vulnerability Assessments; Avoiding Common Mistakes and Liability, Michael Goldsmith.

www.isaca.org, Timothy L. Williams, CPP, Vice President of Corporate and Systems Security for Nortel Networks. member of the ASIS International Board of Directors.

Ira Somerson, CPP

With over 45 years of experience, Ira Somerson, CPP, has originated strategies in risk assessment, security system design, crime prevention, foreseeability studies, security awareness, executive protection, crowd control, fraud prevention, and the development of security management training and orientation curricula. He founded and operated a security company providing security guard resources, crowd control services, alarm system installations, security consulting and services, central station alarm monitoring, and special business investigations for more than 20 years.

He is a recognized lecturer, an authoritative leader, and innovator in the security management profession. His articles have been published extensively. He has lectured frequently at the Wharton School of Business, University of Pennsylvania, and at St. Joseph's University. He formerly taught security courses at Temple University and West Chester University. He is currently on the Editorial Advisory Boards of *Security Journal*, published in Association with the ASIS Foundation by Perpetuity Press, Leicester, UK; the *College Security Report*, Rusting Publications; and *Security Management Bulletin*, Bureau of Business Practices.

Since 1989, Mr. Somerson has maintained a relational database of all consulting and expert witness assignments. He is listed with international and professional directories under the following: Security Systems Expert; Crime and Loss Prevention; Premises Security Liability; Security Officer Consulting; Crowd Control, Expert Witness Security; Security Procedures Development; Security Awareness Programs; Security Training; Foreseability Analysis; and Security Systems Consultant.

Index

retail, 30–31
terrorism, 40–42
violent incident investigation, 39–40
workplace violence, 38–39
prior incident data, 22–23
Private Security (LEAA), 8
productivity, operational impact, 24

Q

qualitative
    analysis, 13
    incident reporting, 116
    methodology, 20
    performance measurement, 121–122
    risk assessment, 14, 20
quantitative
    analysis, 13
    incident reporting, 116
    methodology, 20
    performance measurement, 121–122
    risk assessment, 14, 20–21
    terrorism risk assessment, 41–42

R

Rand Report, 8
reactive vs. pro-active security programs, 10
recovery values, 114
replacement costs, 24
reports
    distribution, 118
    dynamic query, 119
    incident classification, 118
    incident items, 119
    incident loss, 118–119
    incident management, 119
    incident yearly/quarterly/monthly, 119
    incident/event profile, 118
    outcome, root cause, 119
    standard, 117
research reports, 22
responding agencies, 112
risk(s)